A+ goes out to Michelle Davidson for this beautiful account of God's love that she has shared with the world in this book. Her transparency about her life, feelings, and experiences as she came to discover herself as the king's daughter is nothing short of inspiring. Through the use of her own life stories as an example, she truly will encourage anyone who reads this book that God's love is real, and it is for you too.

—Elite Gacin

The King's Daughter is brutally and unflinchingly honest. The book will take you on an emotional roller coaster. You will cry, not only because the stories are real and raw but because you see yourself or someone you know in her words. She was so vulnerable and real and shared more than most are willing to. You will laugh with her to the point people will think that you're insane. But the most beautiful part of this wonderfully written book is the fact that no matter what she went through, she made sure to always put God first and *honor* him every step of her life. I can't wait to see all the lives this book will touch and change. It certainly touched my life and the way I see myself as *The King's Daughter.*

—Swailaine D.

ISBN 979-8-88540-726-7 (paperback)
ISBN 979-8-88540-727-4 (digital)

Christian Faith Publishing
832 Park Avenue
Meadville, PA 16335
www.christianfaithpublishing.com

Printed in the United States of America

THE KING'S DAUGHTER

DIVINELY ORCHESTRATED

Michelle Davidson

For I know the plans and thoughts that I have for you,
says the Lord, plans for peace and well-being and not
for disaster, to give you a future and a hope.

—Jeremiah 29:11 (AMP)

My name, Michelle, means *"who is like the Lord."* It is the feminine form of the Hebrew name Michael: *"who is like God"* or *"a gift from God."* But if anyone had attempted to chart my future trajectory by simply looking at my birth and the early experiences of my life, it would be far from encouraging. In my native country of Liberia (West Africa), respect and acceptance were based on wealth and status. Access and opportunity were gained from the family name, reputation, and education.

Contents

o you trust God enough to follow His plan for your life? Oftentimes, we move with the best of intentions and the sincerest motives. We say yes to the Lord at the most vulnerable moments of our lives, and it is our goal to make a genuine commitment to following His plan, His agenda, His reason for creating us. And then confusion or internal desires overshadow our intentions. When do we get to the place of true and total surrender?

These are difficult questions to answer but are worthy of reflection. "It's so hard, God. I don't know what You are telling me to do. How can I be certain I am hearing You clearly?" I can identify with the internal struggle within your spirit. I have been there until I decided that I was going to trust God even when I could not trace Him.

As a young girl, I was intimately acquainted with trauma. Physically and sexually abused for a seven-year period, amid my pain, I received a beautiful gift of the Good News Bible when I was in the second grade. I gravitated to the red words, and the Holy Spirit beckoned me to trust God. The primary lesson I learned since a little girl is simple. When God created you, He declared you to be very good, and even under the most heinous of circumstances, He envisioned you fulfilling the plan that will allow you to prosper and not be harmed. When you come into alignment with His will for your life, the grand plan begins to unfold. It does not mean tribulation will not occur, but it provides you comfort that God is with you as you navigate through the corridors of life.

This is what I appreciate about *The King's Daughter*. The author, Michelle Davidson, endured significant trauma early in life, and then she met the Lord. She decided to love God and follow His plan for her life, even if it didn't align with her personal goals and objectives. Through her journey, she began to realize His vision for her drastically surpassed anything she could have ever envisioned for herself. She unpacks pivotal moments of her life, the emotions she experienced during bouts of indecision, and her appreciation that He always reminded her that she was in the safest place, when she abided in His Word.

This book will make you reflect. You may shed a tear or two, and you will find yourself celebrating every transformative moment as Michelle pulls back the veil and allows you intimate insight of her relationship with God the Father. Most importantly, I believe her life narrative will encourage you, the reader, to trust God enough to pursue His plan for your life. She leaves nothing to chance; as He has declared, you will uncover the plan when you search for Him with your whole heart. If you are uncertain, insecure about what you believe, you will be capable of reading Michelle's story and gain insight on which direction you can take in your own journey to live your life according to God's plan.

—Rev. Dr. Nicole B. Simpson, CFP
Author, *Dare 2 Dream: Pushing Past Your Pain to Pursue Purpose*
Featured guest, *ABC News*, "9/11 + 20: The Longest Shadow"
Featured guest, *CNN Live* and *BBC World News*
Featured, *Associated Press News*
Two-page feature, *Black Enterprise*
Profiled, *HuffingtonPost.com* and *Crain's New York Business*
President, Generation X Community Association Inc.
732-377-2024
NicoleBSimpson.com
Nicole@NicoleBSimpson.com

Chapter 1

LIFE PRESERVED YET WOUNDED

In my mother's junior high school years, she attended the Totota Lutheran Mission School, a boarding institution in Bong County, Liberia. There she met my father, who was also a student and from a very prominent family. My grandfather was very uncomfortable with their friendship and discouraged my mother from pursuing it any further. In 1970, they graduated from junior high school and moved to Monrovia, Liberia's capital city. My mother enrolled at St. Teresa's Convent, a prominent all-girls school, and my father at St. Patrick's High School, also a prestigious all-boys school. Despite the resistance of my grandfather to their relationship, they continue to see each other.

My mother's family was poor and lived in the Fiamah, Sinkor, area of the capital city. There, all other struggling families shared a latrine and bathhouse built by my grandfather George Marsh. Education was vital to a better future, and parents sacrificed all they could to send their children to the best schools. Thus, my grandfather converted an old refrigerator into an oven to bake and sell a variety of goods to pay his children's tuition, commonly referred to as "school fees." Things turned worse when my grandfather fell gravely ill. My mother, though attending this prestigious school, had to take the local bus route carrying baked goods prepared with fried fish to sell to her classmates for her tuition and other household needs.

My mother and father's relationship continued, and he even met my uncle and some of the family members. By her senior year of high school, she got pregnant. Based on the insistence of my grandfather, my mother dropped out of school. She never shared news of her pregnancy with my father since she was told that he and his family would not accept her or the baby because they were from a prominent, wealthy, and influential family.

My mother was just nineteen years of age and, in her despair, ingested various concoctions to abort the pregnancy, but all attempts failed. Young, scared, alone, my mother was living through hopelessness and uncertainty yet presented with signs of promise and possibilities through those she encountered while pregnant. My strict grandfather had fallen ill to diabetes, struggled with very little money to care for the current family, and was now faced with the financial responsibilities of caring for another child. Concerned with my grandfather's reaction, my mother regularly hid in the home and eventually left to live with a close girlfriend and her mother for some time.

Eventually, my grandfather would bring my mother back home to finish the term of her pregnancy. Upon her return home, a young boy about ten living next door would regularly visit her each day during her pregnancy. His name was Michael, and he brought so much joy to my mother that she loved him with all her heart.

At my birth, the nurse helping with the delivery would emphatically state the special gift she saw on the child. The young boy Michael, who I believe now was an angel sent by God, would spend a few more years visiting mother and child before leaving the area but left a lasting impression on my mother.

So she named me Michelle. It is not a typical name for an African girl, but Michael's friendship and visitation inspired her. Shortly after I was born, my mother would marry a very abusive man, a union that almost cost her her life. It was during this time that Emmanuel Berry, a prominent lawyer in the country I knew at the time to be my father, sent my mother and me to relatives in the United States during personal challenges and the political unrest caused by the civil war after the assassination of President William Tolbert. The country's state was hostile with scarce food and other resources as the military enforced a strict curfew.

When my mother and I arrived in the US, we were both undocumented and lived in a tough housing community in Brooklyn, New York. Frequently, I had to jump over individuals strung out on drugs lying in the streets. And by the time I was six years old, I was watching drug deals happening in the hallway of our building. I got accustomed to staying in our apartment alone after school while my mother worked until midnight. The absence of a strong father figure and the impact of poverty on my life and my mother's as she struggled to keep things together in her twenties resulted in undeniable strongholds that created barriers to a better life.

In the midst of these dire circumstances, an incident with a male family member caused me to feel very uncomfortable at the age of eight. I reported the incident expecting outrage, but the response was very different than what I expected. This individual was a religious figure. I was told it was a figment of my imagination, but it felt and remained a very real experience to me. Pastors and those in religious positions were highly respected in my family. I was left feeling so vulnerable, feeling as though I had no protection. I had no advocate, and I learned at that young age not only the need to fight for myself but also the need to no longer be my animated and joyous self because I may be giving the wrong perception of wanting that type of attention. I became emotionally guarded, a mechanism of defense so that people couldn't figure me out almost to the point that people couldn't see me anymore.

Because I was a child who was not told I was beautiful but instead told that I was ugly, validation was needed and missing in my life. So the first man who approached me and said to me that I was beautiful gave the most sacred thing away because I had no affirmed identity and was hungry for approval. From thirteen, my adolescence was marred by frequent visits to nightclubs, carrying fake IDs, and being in relationships with much older men.

Looking back now, I realize that teenage pregnancy could have been my portion. I could have been a dropout, but I held on to the fact that although I was told that I wasn't beautiful, I was smart. My stepfather, the late Stanley Dunbar, who was introduced in my life around the age of eight, always celebrated how smart I was, which kept me focused on academics. Even though the education most times was not of the best quality, I was determined to make it.

The identity I embraced was formulated by the words I heard that fed my soul. Words have the power to impact the course of life. We are daily afforded the ability to speak life or death (Proverbs 18:21). What I was told and believed became opposing forces in my life, resulting in a poor self-image masked by the diligent pursuit of society's standard of success. My academic success hid the wounds of my past. Thus, many people viewed me as a confident, successful, inspiring leader, to the point I was envied at times.

Chapter 2

TRANSITION THROUGH BROKENNESS

My sister Tamar: King David's daughter

Life can hit you so unexpectedly that it sucks the wind from beneath your wings. In the case of King David's daughter Tamar, the vile act she experienced at the hands of her stepbrother silenced her for life and imprisoned her future (2 Samuel 13). She was left to deal with the trauma and disgrace of being raped and violated by her stepbrother then thrown out in her fragmented state to face the world without any recourse for what happened to her.

Because of the guilt of her father, King David, after arranging the death of his own soldier Uriah to cover the sin of impregnating his wife, Bathsheba (2 Samuel 11), there was no reprimand of son Amnon in defense of his daughter Tamar. We neither hear nor see Tamar again after this encounter. The actions of another rewrote her story and shattered the hope within. How do you get up again, face the world, dream again, trust again?

Considering my circumstances and environment, I didn't view myself as having the luxury of a decision to stay down. Life happens to the innocent and the guilty. Like Tamar and the personal experiences of my life, we must know that we still own our response. Will I choose to stop living and surrender to a life of brokenness and despair or reach for the narrow glimpse of light piercing through the dark hole I found myself buried in? Unless you've been there, it's hard to articulate the raging daily battle happening in the mind of a wounded heart and soul.

Deep down, I dreamt of a future very different from my *current* reality and carried the burden to ensure my better life. I was in crowded spaces, living with strangers at times based on our circumstances, yet very alone. Forming meaningful friendships was problematic due to the many moves we had to make to survive. Yet in every environment I found myself in, someone was there to point out the leadership and good they saw in me. It gave me fragmented hope that fed the escape of my reality vicariously through television programs like *The Cosby Show* and *Diff'rent Strokes*, thinking I could buy my way to the happiness I desired to experience. From the time I was seven, I used television as my guide to possible career paths that would deliver my family out of poverty, healing the tension and stress, allowing us just to love and support each other. We were living in a crisis, where it's human nature to shift to survival mode and do what is deemed necessary to withstand the threat being experienced.

Looking at me, you would have seen a regular teenage girl, yet my life was toxic. All I had consumed mentally and emotionally was deteriorating me from the inside out. It was like being in a sealed room with minimum fresh air circulation, no windows, and no survival instructions. It was in that place that I had to figure out how to survive and not be destroyed by all I had consumed. There were times that the pains of my life were so intense that it would manifest in violent rage or just a flood of tears feeling hopeless.

I was hemorrhaging and surrounded by opinions and individuals that saw my experiences as regular or standard. Where is this internal void coming from that's influencing my expectations? Who am I to want more than that hand I've been dealt? Does someone like me qualify for more than my circumstances? I'm torn yet trying to live.

I was soon known as the emotional *crybaby* of the family. I would write numerous letters to my strong African mother and had to learn to cope with the lack of response. Did she care? Did she understand the deep hurt I was carrying? Another attempt…yet no response.

The letters continued for years, with every stroke, hopeful for a different response yet silence or ridicule for sharing my emotions. Could I earn the expressions of love I yearned to experience? I was a great student, took care of the home, and cared for my younger siblings yet no response. I would go through adolescence and young adulthood with my mind and emotions still stuck in that tight room, gasping for air and bleeding internally. I could handle the disappointment received from the world but had difficulty pushing past the hurt caused by my family.

Masking wounds

I purposed in my heart that I would be successful. Merriam-Webster defines success as a favorable or desired outcome such as achieving wealth, respect, or fame. I could do this! I am smart and could make it happen for myself. My dress, speech, focus, drive, and preparation would put me in a position to be successful. Like a starring role in a blockbuster motion picture, I had to give my best performance to receive the breakthrough I desperately desired. I had to become that person the world identified as successful. It established the framework for my value proposition that clearly defined priorities and relationship standards.

Self-talk was inevitable, considering the wounds I was still carrying from my past. "Michelle, get it together! You can't show everyone how you hurt. You are setting yourself up to be used and taken advantage of. You must be tougher than this. Don't ignore the warning signs. He's not serious, focused, tough, and broke. What could he possibly offer you?"

I dressed well, spoke well, and relentlessly guarded the life I was creating. I recall my mother's sentiments concerning young men that I would introduce to her to always be one of concern that I would once again end ties with them. If I identified signs of abuse, lack of ambition, weakness, or any other factor challenging the vision and mission established, I chose not to waste my time. It had less to do with them and all to do with masking my own insecurities and poor self-image, resulting from failed relationships and trauma I was still carrying in life.

Need for a Savior: The breakdown

The actions of a few religious leaders that I experienced as a child stained my impression of church and my desire for any form of fellowship. My experience at eight years old remained an open wound that never healed and experienced no closure. That and the infamous pastor regularly mentioned by my family, who would have the wife on one side of the church and the girlfriend on the other, deprecated the church for me.

I made it out of my hood and was accepted into a whole new world at the University of Maryland–College Park. It was there that I was asked regularly to attend church services and programs. I often responded, "I'm not interested in attending any church services. There are too many hypocrites there." After many requests, I agreed to go with a friend Gail to a morning service to stop the consistent nagging.

It was near Prince George's Plaza that I would enter this storefront church and sit as the pastor delivered a Word releasing the presence of *God* that would fill the room and draw me into an encounter I had never experienced before. For the first time in over six years, I would cry publicly as the pains and memories of my past would encompass me. Yet I felt safe to be expressive, not entirely understanding what I was experiencing and why I was crying uncontrollably. That first visit would lead to many more visits, altering the desires of my heart and plans after graduation. I received Jesus in my heart and began to experience a change in perspective that some found humorous, including the boyfriend at the time.

In hindsight, the decision to attend school in Maryland far exceeded academic standards and socialization. A divine appointment awaited me, responding to the many letters written over the years to my mother to address the pains I carried since I was a child. I was now entering my senior year, and something new was happening in me. Although that sinful nature was still alive and well due to a lack of understanding, revelation, and transformation, I felt a change that caused me to reconsider my actions and decisions. The clear road map created after interning for years in the Wall Street area and with a boyfriend awaiting my return to New York after graduation became foggy.

Shift in plans

I entered my senior year of college and worked hard to position myself for the next phase of life. After interning for three years in the Wall Street area for an international company, a position was created for me. I would be reporting directly to top executives of a Fortune 500 company. I rarely returned home to Providence, Rhode Island, because of my school and work schedule but decided to make it home the Christmas of 1998. After seeing the living conditions of my mother and younger siblings, I couldn't imagine going on with my life in New York and leaving my hardworking mother and young siblings behind. Only God can explain my call to the top operations executive of my upcoming position to inform him that I had to decline the offer and move back to Rhode Island to help my family.

I made the same call to my long-standing boyfriend residing in New York to his astonishment. There was something different happening in me that changed my processes and redirected my steps. I was that little girl again, dreaming of ensuring a brighter future for my family and willing to sacrifice for the desired outcomes, even if it meant coming back to Rhode Island, the place I vowed never to return to based on the experiences during my two years of high school in this state.

Tempted to fail

I've made some of the most challenging decisions in my adult life for the sake of others with great expectations. Could I now step in and be the coparent to my younger siblings after their father's passing while they were still babies? Could I help give my mother the financial security and life I desired for her since a child?

I'm now back in Rhode Island and expecting to quickly secure a job at the age of twenty-one and being told that I was *overqualified* or that they "don't have the budget to compensate me." With every professional rejection and negativity I was also experiencing at home, I began to firmly doubt my decision to give up the opportunity in New York and return home. The choices I made in that season of my life drastically changed the course of my future. Did I make the right choice? I made the decision to receive Jesus into my heart and now am a child of God, yet my life seems to be worse than before.

God came to this world in the form of man and demonstrated how to win in the face of adversity. Jesus, God in the flesh, was publicly baptized and received the Holy Spirit like you and me, exemplifying the source of our strength and divine guidance we have in this world (Luke 3:21–22). After His public acceptance of life with the Father, He was tempted after fasting forty days without food and drink in the wilderness (Luke 4:1–2).

When you're at your lowest point and on the brink of your breakthrough, like Jesus, we are all placed in the valley of decision, tempting us to lean on our own understanding, but we must decide to stand. In that place, I found a Bible-teaching church and began to seek after the answer to the question of what it meant to be "a child of God." Soon after, I attempted to revisit the nightclubs and discovered I could no longer tolerate the environment. The girlfriends whom I frequented the clubs with, then attended church on Sundays, began to scatter, and we lost touch. Meanwhile, at home, I was ostracized by the very people I sacrificed all to help.

By the time I was twenty-six, I had owned property, and I decided to take my brother to live with me, hoping to give him the life and focus I knew his deceased father would have wanted for him.

He was that stepfather who rewarded me for good grades and talked to me about my future potential. Despite the good happening in my life and my working hard to help my mother, I was still battling the lack of response from her regarding the wounds I still carried, leaving no closure to a tough chapter of my life.

I continued to invest time and resources to pour into my brother sacrificially, but it just was never good enough for my mother. I sincerely asked God, "How could this be my mother?" I desired to be somehow removed from this family. How could someone know of the hurt of their child and do nothing about it? I wanted no part of her in my life moving forward and often cried myself to sleep.

SHIFT IN MINDSET

Appointment with God

Every morning of my life, I wake up early to spend time with *God*, affectionately called my Father, typically followed by a Christian program I use to watch daily. When you set an appointment that you cherish and honor with the Father, He faithfully meets you in that place.

The next morning after my emotional episode concerning my mother, I would hear the host of the television program while faintly listening to her interpret a dream shared by a good friend Quiana and the conversation I just had with the Father that night. She clarified in that one sitting the fact that we do not wrestle with flesh and blood but rather spiritual wickedness in high places (Ephesians 6:10–12). She mentioned a familiar spirit trying to torment the person listening, scheming to derail their destiny.

In the days to come, I would stumble onto the story of Mephibosheth in the book of 2 Samuel 4:4. In the presence of God, I received great revelation about the nurse in that chapter. She had cared for Mephibosheth since his birth and learned of the death of King Saul and son Johnathan in one day: King Saul happened to be the grandfather and Jonathan, the father of the child. All leaders had fled Israel, and this nurse was left in her time of despair to care for the child in the midst of war. In her present state, she did the best she knew how and hastily picked up the child in her fragile state of mind to escape to safety. In her panicked state, attempting to run away to safety, Mephibosheth was dropped and would remain lame for the rest of his life.

While still in her twenties, my beautiful mother left the only country she knew at a time of civil war to come to a foreign land with the hope of providing her daughters a life she didn't have. She worked odd jobs from morning to night to ensure we had a place to live. I recall a time being sick, and she had to ask around for five dollars to purchase medication and items I needed. Although we were struggling, she worked hard to pay for a plane ticket to ensure my sister Tina did not get lost in the circumstances of life poor girls experienced in Liberia.

It is the incorruptible Word of God to honor your mother and father for which the Lord promises a reward of long life and blessings released upon you (Exodus 20:12, Leviticus 19:3, Ephesians 6:2). The contrary leads to setbacks and curses (Exodus 21:17) undone only through a repented heart. In the presence of God, my spiritual sight was sharpened to see my mother through new lenses. She was a woman also fighting through the rejected wounds of her past, intending the best in her present state. I was clouded by my own pain and struggled to value her expressions of love delivered in the form of shelter, food, and hard work. The enemy of my soul planned to see me curse and reject my mother, derailing my destiny and future. But God came to my rescue in the flesh, raising up a standard against him through my acceptance of Jesus as Lord and final authority of my life (Isaiah 59:19).

It was in the presence of God that I learned to love my mother unconditionally. Expressing verbally, "I love you," with hugs, wanting nothing more than for her to feel appreciated. It took some time for my heart to catch up with my physical actions, recognizing I was still wounded. Despite how I felt, I vowed to honor God's instructions.

Approximately three months later, I would receive a call from my mother that speaks to the power of love to heal the heart and restore what seemed lost. She had visited three businesses that day and kept running into people I had helped in the community. Each time, they celebrated her for a job well done with raising me and expressed how proud she must be to have me as her daughter. It brought her to a place of tears that led her to make the long-awaited call to express how much she loved me and how I have made her so proud over the years.

What I longed for over the years and experienced from my mother that day was something I had to first freely give. We don't know how life's experiences have impacted those we love or encounter and tend to hold expectations of how we believe we ought to be treated but have learned the power of giving that releases abundance of what we desire to receive. Agape, the love that comes from the Father, is unconditional, patient, kind, not self-seeking, not easily angered, and keeping no record of the wrongs that occurred (1 Corinthians 13: 4–5). The love of God has the power to destroy darkness and bring forth restoration in every area of life. My heart sings of my joy and gratitude, understanding in the darkest hours of my life—although I didn't see Him, not sure I even felt Him—He was my help, protector, and provided (Jeremiah 29:11). As I gave love, I received an abundance of love, healing, restoration, and peace.

Chapter 4

GREATER CAPACITY TO LOVE

Salvation

To be loved in my current condition, seeing past my mistakes, and being overwhelmingly embraced with no consideration of my race, education, family status, financial condition, citizenship, job title, or ethnicity challenges my natural mind but edifies the Spirit of God dwelling in me. Imagine a parent watching his child falling and struggling, trying to complete a task with no guidance and instruction yet knowing that the child simply needs the love, support, and clear demonstration on how to achieve what's been a difficult challenge for some time.

When seeing the potential of their children, most parents seek to encourage and provide the best support they can for their development. As parents, with our own imperfections, if we desire to give the very best to our children, what more the Father, our Creator (Matthew 7:11)? The Father didn't wait on our request. Instead, He came in the flesh to meet us right where we are (John 1:14), to stretch out His loving arms, support, and demonstrate how to overcome and crush every obstacle we face in life. You see, it's not that

I can't; instead, show me how. Give me the freedom needed to try while firmly encouraging my development.

Why did He come? We were created in His image and likeness with the freedom of choice to make the decisions that support life and death (Genesis 1:26–27). As children, we are impressionable, which can lead to poor choices. The rebellious decision of the first humans, Adam and Eve, was sin that led to the spiritual death of all mankind (Genesis 2:16–17). Although it may be warranted, do we allow our children to be destroyed or harmed when we are in a position to help them? Emphatically, no! Jesus, God in the flesh, came to rescue each of us from spiritual death and a defeated life that we may experience the depth of His unconditional love and compassion (2 Corinthians 5:17–21).

It is okay to fail! Just don't stay there. There are many rounds in a fight and the battle designed to see you quit or defeated. My defeat yesterday does not erase the hope in the victory for today. We are reconciled and embraced by the Father, who took every sin committed and placed them on the back of Jesus, making us whole again.

He loves us to the point of death (Romans 5:8). Like our children, we can never be good enough to earn His love (Ephesians 2:8). As He redeemed our lives, He healed us from our past, sickness, and diseases (Isaiah 58:8). All He asks is that we consider our actions, choose to acknowledge our mistakes, sincerely apologize for the wrongs that we have committed, and receive the freedom released by His divine grace (Romans 3:24). Like you, I am not excluded based on my past. I instead embrace my new day, understanding like that a child learning to develop new skills, I have the firm support and love of my Father.

Intimacy: saved and redeemed

Father, before I even knew You, the Bible says, You knew me (Jeremiah 29:11). Your plans were to prosper me and do me no harm, to give me a future and expected end. So You knew the path that I would take in life, knew the areas of suffering and pain, but You also sent me the answer. You placed Your hand in the pit, and

You came to get me. You knew the mistakes and wrong decisions, yet You found it fit to send Jesus to pull me out of the pit of despair I found myself in. Drowning in my tears and sorrows, alive yet not living. You came in the flesh (John 1:14) and pulled me out of the pit and fiery furnace and redeemed my life. You placed fresh oil upon my head (Psalm 92:10) and strengthened my feet like hinds' feet (Habakkuk 3:19) so I may tread upon the serpent and adder and trample them under my feet. Father, it comes down to this: how do I push forward and embrace the redemption, the compassion, peace, and the supernatural strength released upon my life as the righteous through Christ Jesus (2 Corinthians 5:21)?

As this prayer is released, it is up to us to receive the Word of the Lord in Romans 8, which expresses to a believer the liberation from all condemnation for those that have received Christ Jesus as Lord of their lives receiving freedom from sin and death. I know what it is to be freed yet firmly bound by my thinking, stuck in the reality of my past, and fearful of change. I'm reminded of the 1994 drama film entitled *The Shawshank Redemption*, where the elderly prisoner Brooks Hatlen, established as a librarian in prison with many friends, was granted parole in his old age. Receiving the news of his freedom, he made every attempt to overturn his release, fearful of a world he hadn't experienced for fifty years.

As a freedman, he struggled with living free and socializing again. He would eventually take his own life soon after. His inmate friend Ellis Boyd "Red" Redding would soon be released after spending forty years in prison. Although Red also experienced some of the emotions of his friend Brooks, he had a life-changing encounter with a fellow escaped inmate Andy Dufresne that changed his perspective on life and freedom. As a freedman, he broke free from the mundane routine of life and decided to live again courageously.

Our mind is a battlefield, and how we choose to think and execute will determine the access and opportunities awaiting us. The cell door has been opened with no guards or barbed wire fence hindering our progress. The problem is that we can become institutionalized, conformed to slavery, bondage, lack, and abuse. Anything outside of the normal we have embraced is scary, challenging, uncertain. There is death and life in the power of the tongue (Proverbs 18:21). The transformation of our thinking that shatters our mind's limitations is produced in what we say concerning ourselves and what we choose to believe.

I had to decide to receive my redemption and make up my mind to stop valuing myself based on my yesterday and even the mistakes I'll make today. Jesus is the open door that leads to a life we were fearful to dream with the assurance found in the Word of God of divine abundance (John 10:7–10). We will never be bad enough to be excluded from this promise. The open door awaits the destitute, the broken, the unqualified, the misunderstood, the perfectionist, the deceived, the person needing a compassionate embrace of a Father.

Cured in His presence

Coming from the world and the life that I lived, I refused, after my years of college, to have an encounter with God then go into the church and treat it as though it was an ICU. A place to get medicated, endure for a few hours, feel better about myself, it wears off, and I return to the same state I was in prior. The Word of God and time spent in the presence of the Holy Spirit are healing for me and cure the pains of my heart. He was the cure to the ill thoughts in my mind. He was the cure to that void I felt in life. He was the answer.

That time and intimacy with the Holy Spirit were developed in His presence. It was cultivated through a time of intimacy in His Word, receptive to transparency and vulnerability. In that time, the Father touched every aspect of my life and began to create a new heart and a new spirit within me as a born-again believer (Ezekiel 36:26). It was okay to share my tenderness, cheerful spirit, and compassionate love. It allowed me to change my posture and fight with appropriate weapons. I no longer had to be my provider of every need, the protector of my life, and medicate for my healing. I had the privilege of getting to know God as *Jehovah Jireh* (my provider), *Jehovah Nissi* (my banner-victory), and *Jehovah Rapha* (my healer), willing and able to preserve me in every situation. His power is manifested in my life through the sword of the Spirit, the Word of God spoken in every situation I face (Ephesians 6:17).

In my intimate language understood by God, I pray from my Spirit, like a child learning to speak new words that are clearly interpreted in the presence of parents. Through that intimate encounter in prayer, my Father responds to all kinds of prayers and requests (Ephesians 6:18). That place of intimacy destroys yokes standing as a stronghold suppressing your deliverance, healing, lifting, and turnaround. Jesus is the antidote that counteracts the poisonous life we've lived. I spent years holding my antidote as a churchgoer and following the lead of others, thinking that was the extent of salvation.

God desires to do exceedingly, abundantly, above all we could ever ask or think (Ephesians 3:20). When my expectations began to align itself with the Word of God and push forward with shaking needs to obey the instructions received in His presence, I began to experience the power of the antidote from my poisonous past, learning with every step taken how to live as a cured woman healed in the presence of God.

Chapter 5

IDENTITY

Demonstration of the process

We have all come to a place where we battled with what we knew was right and what we have seen demonstrated. Throughout my childhood and adolescence, I've experienced trauma that stood as opposition to walking with the Lord, stemming from the crass behavior seen in the lives of those that I watched. They proclaimed with their lips to be saved, to be sanctified, and carried titles of pastors, of spiritual leaders like prophets of God, yet they were manipulative and, in some cases, adulterers. So the examples and the demonstration of their lives began to formulate in me a perception of what could be, which was extremely limited.

The Word of God in the book of Luke, chapter 3, verse 16, the Bible says that as the people were baptized by John the Baptist, Jesus Himself was baptized also. He came to be the ultimate example. He came to show us how to win, how to embrace the presence of God. How to endure the temptations of this world? Like Jesus in the book of Luke, chapter 4, after He was baptized and the Spirit of the Lord descended upon Him, the Bible says He was led into the desert for forty days without any food and drink. During this period, He was tempted by the devil.

So many of us have made that declaration of our salvation, and like Jesus, I was tempted right after I made the decision to live a redeemed life. Looking at my wonderful children, I can't help but reflect upon the deception of the devil, lurking as a prowler to steal, kill, and destroy (John 10:10).

After receiving Jesus as Lord and Savior of my life, I went to a routine doctor's appointment. During that appointment, I was advised that I would need a hysterectomy based on an exam and X-rays. I was in my early twenties, and this drastic procedure would make the ability to have children impossible.

Have you been tempted? What lies have the enemy fed you that cause you to derail, to abort the plan of God for your life? I remember driving home that day full of despair, although I had just received Jesus as Lord of my life. I thought to myself, *How I turned from the life I used to live, and now that I confess to being a child of God through salvation, how could this be my portion? How could this be my fate?*

As I cried the tears that could fill a river while trying to drive home, I was led to call my late grandmother Elizabeth. It was during that call that my grandmother was the voice of God in my ear. "Get a hold of yourself!" she said. "You are a child of God now."

It was that divine encouragement that helped me make it home that day. It helped me begin the journey that I've been on for over twenty years, answering the question of what it means to be a child of God—learning to embrace what God has done already for me if I choose to believe and take Him at His Word.

We are all tempted to abort, to distort the word of God in our lives. We are pushed to limits that, in our own strength, are impossible. We can choose to surrender our will, our life, and make that choice to trust His Word as the final say. God's Word is unwavering, even through the most difficult trials and temptations.

My best friend: the Holy Spirit

One of my favorite movies as a child was *The Karate Kid* starring Ralph Macchio as Daniel LaRusso as the student and Pat Morita as Mr. Miyagi, his coach and trainer. Daniel, along with his single mother, moved from Newark, New Jersey, to Los Angeles, California, to start a new life. It is there that his life takes a turn for the better when he starts dating Ali Mills.

But this also gained him enemies from the karate club Cobra Kai as Ali's ex-boyfriend was jealous about Daniel's association with Ali. Daniel became the object of random attacks because of his association with Ali. After almost losing his life in an ambush by the Cobra Kai, Daniel was rescued by Mr. Miyagi, who would then become his trainer.

In Daniel's training, he was introduced to activities and chores, such as painting, that he deemed irrelevant to karate and at times resisted the training process introduced. It wasn't until the end of the movie that he awoke to the revelation of the importance of the mental capacity to win, the resources available for his deliverance, and the value of every aspect of his training not always associated with karate. Our tasks in life, if well received, transform our thinking and cultivate the discipline needed to win.

We are daily awakening to new horizons that take us down so many paths in life, and oftentimes, we need a compass to direct our path and strengthen our journey. Before a renewed life through Christ, and even as a woman confessing salvation, I found myself struggling to make it happen in life based on my experiences, emotions, and understanding. The challenges were immobilizing, requiring the need to exert time, resources, and energy I didn't necessarily have. Although declaring salvation, attending, and supporting my local church faithfully, I found myself imbalanced, seeing some progress in certain areas of life while struggling in others.

It is the will of the Father that His children enjoy the wholeness of life in His presence, where nothing is missing, broken, or lacking. Like the guidance, training, and support shown by Mr. Miyagi for Daniel, our Father came to earth in the fleshly form as Jesus to ensure His presence, love, guidance, protection, and divine wisdom manifested in our lives. He is the Spirit of truth, accessible to those who have accepted Him as Father through the confession of Jesus as Lord of their lives.

The Father is so compassionately in love with us that He sent Jesus to dwell in us by the Holy Spirit. Know today that the Holy Spirit is a true person who abides in us (John 14:17). Like any cherished relationship, you exercise care, respect, and communication to ensure the strength of the relationship. I realized through my journey just how patient the Father has been in my life, allowing me the liberty to fall, get up again, yet remain right there to meet me in my current state. When I began to acknowledge His constant presence in my life by the Holy Spirit, the losing battles I tried to fight in my own strength soon began to turn around for my good. He became that blessed assurance that I would inquire of to bring forth the guidance in the decisions of my life. No longer would I have to fear the circumstances trying to attack my peace and progress. Instead, in my intimate time with the Holy Spirit, I received His divine role as an abiding helper sent that I may experience life more abundantly (John 14:26).

He's there on the mountaintop of every victory, at the table in the presence of my enemies, the platforms and stages arranged for the giftings placed on our lives. With trust and reliance, we allow the Holy Spirit to lead us on the path of holistic victory that begins with the renewal of our mind, the healing of our heart, the execution of the divine vision of mission provided by the Father.

Lifetime partner

Salvation through Christ Jesus brought me the greatest friend I'll ever know, a friend who knows every aspect of who I am, knows my falling and my getting up, knows my mistakes even before I make them—and through it all, loves me, adores me, covers me, protects me, comforts me, and edifies me. That friend, that life partner, my greatest friend for life is the Holy Spirit. A person who dwells in this temple, never leaves me nor forsakes me but guides me through this life, through every test, trial, victory, and challenge, the Holy Spirit has been there.

Whether I received Him fully or not, He has been there. As I gave my life to Christ, I also embraced the scripture from the book of

Proverbs chapter 3, verses 5–6: "Trust the Lord with all thine heart; and lean, not on my own understanding. In all your ways, acknowledge Him, and He shall direct thy paths."

When I got saved, I was so used to making things happen for myself. I was so proud of my independence. If I couldn't get it done, it wouldn't get done. And so, when I got saved, my mind had to be renewed to receive the newness of my life, to receive the newness of my helper, a friend, and a keeper like no other. He's the One who could accelerate the things done naturally and take it to heights and levels only dreamt possible. For greater is He, the Holy Spirit in me, than he who is in the world (1 John 4:4). So when I'm aligned and in agreement through our relationship, I go to levels and heights through God that brings acceleration in my workplace, finances, marriage, children, vision, and mission.

I think back to a time when things were so difficult in my marriage. I remember when I met my husband, and I said, "Lord, this looks like a project." I went on a fast for three days. During that time, the Lord, through the Holy Spirit, spoke to me; He showed me my husband. He didn't sugarcoat him; He didn't dress him up. He said this is who he is. These are his areas of weakness. These are the areas of struggle, but he is my choice for you.

Based on my relationship with the Holy Spirit, I cried when he told me that Cliff was His choice. I cried because I saw the process. I saw the pain. I saw the delay and the setbacks but had to trust God with everything that was within me. Will the instructions of God the Father, provided through the Holy Spirit, be the final say in our lives? So if He says this is His choice for me, crying and shaking, I accepted the man who would be my husband, understanding it was going to be a process seeing my husband's areas of deficiencies. What I didn't understand in that process was, as much as God was going to make my husband through it, He was making me as well.

So one year went by. I'm praying. I'm fasting. I believe God, with sparks of change, but no transformation. Year 2, year 3, the setback in year 4, try to get back up in year 5—I continued to push through, continued to cry through, continued to suffer and endure through.

The time came when I just felt that I had enough, and I thought it was time to part our ways. During that time, the Lord used Jeremiah, our son, to speak to my heart and speak to my spirit. There was just this void and grief that I felt. I had sought counsel, and the counsel justified my decision, but I was not reconciled in my spirit that it was time to let go. I was not reconciled with that, for as God reconciled me through Christ Jesus, He has given me the ministry of reconciliation (2 Corinthians 5:18).

It was at that time that I cried out to the Lord. "Lord, what would you have me to do?" I asked. "For I know, I fasted and prayed, and You said this was your choice for me." So many times, we're on the right path, but the turbulence experienced on the journey causes us to abort or change course. I was emotionally unstable due to all I had experienced, yet the Lord's Word for me provided when I fasted and prayed before entering this union had not changed. If I would embrace His process and not grow weary in well doing, I would reap abundantly from His harvest (Galatians 6:9).

It was in that quiet place through the leading of the Holy Spirit that I began to see images and began to see where things went wrong. See, when I got married in my late twenties, I owned properties and was the CEO of my own company. As far as the world's standards, I was doing really well. I had my own money, I had my own home, and I never made room for my husband to feel the love, acceptance, and need I had for him in my life.

The Holy Spirit revealed to me that my husband was a man who didn't feel wanted or needed. I shared with him the need for his children to have him in their life but never deeply shared the need for his wife to have him, love him, and need him. It was in that place after he left the house that I would pick up the phone and leave this message: "I've told you for years that your children needed you, but I need you, and I desire you in my life. I want to spend the rest of my life with you."

Although I felt justified allowing him to leave because I was unreconciled in my spirit, my husband came home, which was a turning point for our marriage. Our life was finally headed on the right course. The experiences I faced in my marriage had less to do with my husband, Cliff, and more to do with the conditions of my heart and the depth of my love walk. Could Michelle be an extension of the Father's love that breaks yokes in our lives and transforms those that encounter His agape love through our lives?

There are so many times that we have aborted God's plan for our life. We have aborted the vision and mission because we missed it in the natural, considering our senses and even the comments or recommendations of good-hearted people. I know undoubtedly that the Holy Spirit is the best friend I could ever have and confidently trust His counsel over my own and the opinions of others.

I've learned through trials and processes that I can firmly trust the Holy Spirit. I can trust his guidance and instruction. I can love as Christ loves and bring forth reconciliation, which is the desire of the Father that we—His people, His daughters and sons—reconcile His people back to Him. They too may live a life that not just glorifies Him but a life also full of joy that comes from Him. So by laying down Michelle's understanding and reasoning and abandoning my understanding, I cried out to the Lord, and I called my husband.

Today, I look in his eyes and thank God for the love that I see for another. I thank God in the name of Jesus for what He's done in my house, what He's doing in my children. I thank God for the man, the leader, the priest firmly developing in God's presence. It is not about me; it's about him and the intimacy with His heavenly Father through the leading of the Holy Spirit. His friend and his partner for life who strengthen and encourage him to lead his house and be revered by his wife to be by his side.

Companionship with the Holy Spirit shall never lead us wrong. It will lead us into the hands and the heart of the Father. It will perfect the things that concern us. It will heal, deliver, and set free. My best friend, the Holy Spirit, has been everything to me. And even the day of my wedding, the first message to the guests in my program was the letter to my first love, my heavenly Father communing with me as the Holy Spirit. My God, my keeper, my waymaker, for You have bought me a mighty long way. It is the way that You choose to take Your sons and daughters.

Are we going to allow the Holy Spirit to have the final say in our lives and the circumstances and situations that we push our way through? Understanding that the Word of the Lord says in the book of 2 Chronicles, chapter 20, verse 15: do not be dismayed, don't be afraid, for the battle is not ours to fight, it is the Lord. As we keep our mind and eye on Him and commune with the Holy Spirit, He orders our steps. He gives us guidance, direction and shields us from the fire to never be burned. Even in the floods, we will not drown, for that friend and helper is with us.

But is He in His rightful place in our life? Is He the one whom we seek first as David regularly inquired of the Lord? He inquired of the Lord (1 Samuel 23:4), and when he did, he was triumphant over every enemy. When King Saul did not seek the Lord's face, he found himself enduring many mistakes, facing loss and despair (1 Chronicles 10:14).

Through everything that my husband and I have endured, we have learned to move in reverence and inquiry of the will of God through the guidance of the Holy Spirit. What would You have us do? You have been a friend, Holy Spirit, like no other, my peace in the midst of a storm. The more I fell in love with You, the more I fell in love with Your leading, understanding that I couldn't do this without You.

The more You shattered every obstacle before me, the more divine turnaround was manifested in my life. You are the answer. You are the answer to life victorious in God. You are the answer to every dream, to every vision. Holy Spirit, You have been my answer. You have been my friend. You have been my companion. You have been my judge. You have been my jury. You have been the one to correct me. You have been the one to perfect God in me continuously. I'm grateful. I'm grateful for Your presence. I'm thankful for Your love. I'm thankful for Your peace. I am thankful for Your friendship. I am grateful for the healing that I have experienced in Your presence.

Holy Spirit, where would I be without You? How can any of us who proclaim to be believers thrive in a life that You do not lead? Our friendship and partnership bring us such victory, joy, and peace for the rest of our days. I'm committing this life and life more abundantly in Your presence.

Imperfect I am, but Your grace remains sufficient for me (2 Corinthians 12:9). I choose to walk with You and talk with You and allow You to continuously chisel away at my old way of understanding, thinking, speaking, and doing. Through the graceful fire of the living God, I may behold Your creation and experience Your glory in every aspect of my life that our children may know You intimately as they see the examples of their parents that they may walk in reverence of You.

Holy Spirit, thank You for Your friendship today. Thank You for Your love. Thank You for Your compassion. Thank You for all that You've done in my heart and my mind. Thank You for the doors that You've opened that no man was able to close. Thank You for the years that You have restored to me and my husband, Cliff. Thank You for what You've done in our lives.

Holy Spirit, no man can lose with You in the first place, guiding and leading our lives. And for that and forever, we give You praise.

Chapter 6

CHOICES

Frequency of God

Sometimes you must reflect on life and the journey thus far. If we're honest with ourselves, as believers, we can identify the many times we did our own thing, anxious about outcomes and oblivious to the guidance of the Holy Spirit. In the book of Genesis, chapter 15, Abram, a man in his eighties, shared his concerns of being childless and having no children to inherit his estate (2). The Word of the Lord came to him that his offspring would outnumber the stars in the sky (3). Taking matters into her own hands, his wife, Sarai, also older in age and convinced she was cursed by the Lord, suggested to her husband that he lay with her maid Hagar to bring forth the desires of their hearts (2). Although Abram heard from God, he agreed with the plan, and Hagar soon became pregnant and began to despise Sarai, the very woman that put her in her current position (4).

Can we acknowledge that some of the difficulties and trials that we are experiencing are self-imposed? Yes, we heard from God and saw visions of what was to come, but are we lying in His presence, thanking Him for the blessing and asking the Father, through the divine guidance of the Holy Spirit, to order our steps and lead us down His path? I'll be the first to say, the mistakes made at work, in business, managing tenants, financial ventures, marriage, rearing of children, and in other aspects of my life had all to do with not inquiring of the Holy Spirit in my handling of the situation at hand. It led to setbacks, injuries, and bondage, which were avoidable.

We deal with the voices of negative self-talk, others' opinions, the bondage of our past in determining the possibilities of our present. Can we accept the incorruptible fact that God is not a man that He shall lie nor the son of man to renege on the blessings He has revealed to us concerning our lives (Numbers 23:19)? Because of our insecurities and anxiousness, we seek our prompt results through false prophets, palm readers, astrology, and the opinion of others.

How have we derailed our lives by leaning on our understanding that changed the course of our divine destiny? Was that husband or relationship God's choice for you? Is the fact that you're still renting due to your impulsive spending disregarding the stewardship of resources to accomplish homeownership? Was the business established instructed by God or your desires that resulted in failure because of lack of preparation?

Like you, I had to ask myself these questions and accept the truth revealed. It often led to repentance and a deeper level of trust in the safety and victory I have in God through the leading of the Holy Spirit. I recall purchasing two homes, with one being a single-family and the second two-family. Being the owner of both properties, I decided that my household of one would live in the four-bedroom home. My mother consistently expressed the wisdom of moving into the two-bedroom apartment, with ample space for me, but ignored her advice. I would soon find myself in financial difficulty paying for a home on my own and with tenants who were not paying rent on time. The Lord will speak through others to ensure the guidance we need to be successful. The question is, are we operating on His frequency, familiar with the voice of the Holy Spirit to lead us down a path of safety and victory consistently?

God has a set time to manifest the divine promises revealed to us, according to Ecclesiastes 3:11. His ways are not our ways. He knows the development required for us to maximize the blessing at hand. Are our minds renewed, hearts healed and compassionate, skills developed, life put in order to enjoy the elevation desired by God for our lives?

When we think of our children, godchildren, nieces, and cousins, there are many plans and gifts we desire to release into their lives but tend to wait for the appropriate time when they are capable of receiving and maximizing the blessing. The same stands true for our Father in heaven. He loves us enough to examine our present state, guide us to the place of promotion that we may receive His best.

The question I faced that shifted the course of my life was the commitment to grow in the presence of God that I may know His voice, which ensures that I'm operating on His frequency even amid trials and perceived setbacks. I no longer desire to be the boss lady, which comes with having all the answers and figuring out the right course of action. Instead, I'm God's ambassador, representing Him in the places He instructs me to go with the confidence of His endorsement.

I am grateful daily that God is so merciful and receives His children in our present condition, and chooses to fulfill His promises in our lives. In Genesis 17, God revisited Abram over ten years after proclaiming His desire to bless Him with a child that would inherit his estate. Abram would become Abraham, the father of many nations since the child Isaac brought forth from the womb of his wife Sarah would spark the generational blessings of kings and leaders in his lineage. Abraham was ninety-nine years of age when the overflowing promises of God manifested in his life. His wife Sarah, nursing her first child in her old age, said, "God has made laughter for me" (Genesis 21:6).

At times in life, it may seem as though the dream and vision are taking too long to manifest, but know it is always for an appointed time for those who believe and hold steadfast to the Word of God and the instructions provided by the Holy Spirit. Were Abraham and Sarah ready to receive their promise sooner? That's an intimate conversation we must all have with the Father. I know now that my desires for life would have been jeopardized if received sooner in my life. God's faithfulness is inevitable when we are attuned to His voice, guidance, and willingness to execute His instructions.

Loving self

I was spunky, vibrant, expressive, fashionable, and enjoyed dressing up in my mother's high heels as a child, the same high heels that led to the scar I still have on my bottom lip. As the years went by, I would hear comments about my appearance and comparisons with "the pretty one through interactions and circumstances." I was called ugly but always followed up with "but very smart," which would be my saving grace. I went from that vibrant, expressive child who was always modeling in the mirror to having a tough time looking at my reflection. The best designer clothes and accessories became my superficial identity, masking the ugliness I could now see.

After being exploited by charming words that led to poor decisions, I lacked trust for others. But one day, as I watched my regular Christian morning show, I heard the host describe her process of dealing with the insecurities she was battling through. It was from that program that I realized that it all starts with me, not what my mommy or daddy said but what I chose to believe now. I went back to my Creator, who formed me in my mother's womb, and found these words written: "Indeed the very hairs of your head are all numbered. Do not be afraid; you are far more valuable than many sparrows" (Luke 12:7). Every detail of my creation was handcrafted by God, my Father. *He* does all things well.

For five months, I would make an appointment in my bathroom mirror daily to appreciate the reflection I saw. I would compliment my eyes, smile, bone structure, teeth, style, hair, intelligence, laugh, heart for others, and simply for being Michelle, the person. I would praise the Father, for I've been fearfully and wonderfully created by Him (Psalm 139:14). Healing starts with me, my perception of myself, and what I choose to receive.

Forgiving self

My choices in life led to poor decisions that became the ball and chain firmly qualifying me in my mind of who I am and what I could aspire to be. The experiences of poverty and actions faced as a teen determined my net worth and created my walls of limitations. There was so much I accepted as being too good for me. I remember a very nice young man in college who always supported and adored me. When he finally gained the courage to share how he felt, I hooked him up with a nice girl (that I deemed to be more) appropriate for him.

As I continued to work hard, I made progress that changed my financial condition. I gave away more than I retained, feeling unworthy to accumulate certain levels of wealth. The conditions of my heart and mind determined where I could live and who I could become. Did I deserve the desires of my heart? Could a girl like me rise to heights and levels only seen on the big screen and played through my imagination?

In the book of Joshua, chapter 2, we are introduced to the woman Rahab, a harlot running a brothel. Because of her profession, she was considered among the lowest in society, forming grave implications for her future. The heart of Rahab, a woman from a foreign land, was introduced in Joshua chapter 2 as she spoke of the God of the children of Israel with reverence (Joshua 2:11), desiring His mercy on her household. Her requests far outweighed the ambition for material wealth that would be from a woman in her position. Instead, she aspired to save the lives of her father's household and preserve their future (Joshua 2:13).

She was instructed to hang a scarlet cord from her window, marking her home for protection. Like the children of Israel in Exodus 3:9, God sees the heart of people and chooses to accept and protect us right where we are. As the home of God's people was marked with the blood of the lamb in Egypt, ensuring the preservation of life (Exodus 12:13), the scarlet cord hanging from Rahab's window was an extension of His mercy upon the lost. Our past never disqualifies us from the abundant future the Father desires to unfold before us.

It is up to us to courageously choose to receive the forgiveness from our sinful past made possible through a loving God who came to the earth in the form of man (Jesus) and bore every sin on His back that was buried in death and resurrected on the third day, redeeming us from our yesterday (Isaiah 44:22). I am not made worthy through good deeds and acts of kindness. Jesus came that I may be saved and redeemed; He took the guilt of my past and brought forth an abundance of peace, healing, grace, favor, provision, and access (John 10:10). It is available to us all, but can we receive it? The slate has been washed clean, but we tend to battle in our minds the worthiness of receiving such an expensive gift.

Through my walk with the Father, I realized that my acceptance of freedom was in stages, and I had to learn to be free. I come from experiences where you had to work for everything you had, and anything given came with a high price. Could I receive the love of my husband without the thought of manipulation and strings attached? Should I expect to bear children who would one day be world changers? Could I enjoy the abundance of provision derived from my labor without guilt? Could I speak before authority as an influencer of change? Am I worthy of healing and total deliverance in my spirit, soul, and body?

My acceptance of Jesus as Lord and big brother made me the righteousness of God (2 Corinthians 5:21). I have the forgiveness of sin, eternal life, and grace that releases divine favor and abundance through this righteousness. Every year, through the experience of my life, I learned to let go of my understanding and receive more of the blessing that's been there for me all along. I am forgiven and choose to receive my forgiveness! I now courageously love deeper, dream bigger, and expect what seems naturally impossible.

Rahab, the woman once known as a harlot, changed her destiny through the reverence of a compassionate God. He blessed her with a husband, and she would go on to birth a prominent son Boaz and be included in the genealogy that brought forth Jesus, the Christ (Matthew 1). This speaks to the unfailing love of God that is available to all that receive Him. Today, I stand in awe of the healing, blessings, and favor I see in my life, which has only been made possible through the redemption I've experienced through my intimate relationship with the Father, Jesus, and Holy Spirit. I RECEIVE FORGIVENESS!

Encourage self

Life can blindside you with tremendous trials sent to discourage, derail, and paralyze the vision you hoped for. We begin to search for help, hoping for relief from the pains and struggles of our current condition. The spirit of discouragement has raised its head often in our lives, serving as a conviction based on our past and a deceiver that desires us to accept defeat and death.

In the book of 1 Samuel, chapter 30, David, the future king of Israel, was living on the outskirts of a foreign land due to the threat he faced in his own country. As he pushed forward in faith, he and the men he led came back to their camp to learn of a raid by the Amalekites that occurred, and their homes in Ziklag burned, and women were taken captive with all that was with them. Although David and all the men were directly impacted by this raid that took their wives and children, he became the focus of blame, and his once companions thought of stoning him.

Know today that trials will come to destroy the innocent and guilty. The friends you have been leaning on may be the very ones who attack you. Understand, attacks will come to kill the dream that's within you, yet a person who chooses to trust the God of their salvation and demonstrate faith in His unfailing Word will never be defeated (John 16:33). God's presence is the key to your breakthrough, reverencing that He is your Father, deliverer, provider, healer, restorer, and peace. You have to choose to confidently speak the Word in faith over your fears and allow the God of heaven and earth to fight for you (2 Chronicles 20:15). He is a Father like no other, who has the power to resurrect the dead areas of your life and restore what's been broken.

In the midst of despair and isolation, David encouraged himself in the Lord and inquired confidently of Him to provide wisdom and guidance in the situation faced. I can testify of strongholds that were to be brought down but remained standing because I tried to fight in my own strength. I understand now, through all I've faced, the inadequate strength I have facing life alone without the support and guidance of my Father. Loss and pain extended due to the wounds

I continued to feed by my thoughts and actions, instead of starving depression and hurt by the Word I spoke and what I chose to believe.

When you allow the power of the Holy Spirit to transform your mind, sight, heart, and speech, you will operate in the grace that transcends natural understanding. David and the men with him pursued the enemy who had taken everything from them and recovered all (1 Samuel 30:18). Pursue everything that the Lord has spoken through dreams and vision, and expect your victory!

Chapter 7

SPEAK THE WORD

Speak the Word

As believers filled with the Holy Spirit, we fight through prayer for our peace, marriages, children, vision, and provision. Our weapons are not carnal but mighty for the pulling down of strongholds (2 Corinthians 10:4). We speak the Word of God, sing praises to His name, and have confidence in the authority received through Jesus as Lord of our lives. Darkness will never overcome the light (John 1:5), so we rejoice during the trial, confident that we are more than conquerors through Christ Jesus (Romans 8:35–39).

The Word of God edifies, and His presence liberates. When consistently utilized, you become that champion carrying a supernatural sword that defends and preserves the land (Ephesian 6:13–17). Be encouraged! As you confidently speak the Word, worship the Father, and maintain your peace, you will forever stand as a victor and not a victim.

So in despair and uncertainty that are causing the tears to flow, lift up your eyes, heart, and arms to receive the unfailing love of your Father. As you speak the Word of God that He honors above

His name (Psalm 138:2), you will experience the shift in your marriage, children, finances, access, and opportunities. Remain steadfast, immovable, and confident in the power of God to transform your situation. As you continue to exercise your faith, the mountains threatening your home, career, health, and dreams will have no alternative but to be abruptly removed (Mark 11:23). We are made in the image and likeness of the Father and given authority through Jesus to speak the Word by faith and receive the blessings aligned with His Word.

As a single woman, I was proposed to by a nice guy but struggled with the decision of marrying him. I reasoned in my mind the possibilities of success and proceeded with the engagement. I checked off a few items on the checklist, and he made the cut. He was a believer, respectful, hardworking, and family oriented. That decision was not made with the guidance of the Holy Spirit, and I began to lose my peace.

I lifted up my eyes to the Father and repented for going before Him and asked that He guide me out of this situation. Although I knew the marriage wouldn't go forth, I had to trust the timing of God to guide me safely out of the entanglement I caused. I would go months with no change but continue to keep my eye on the one who held all power in His hands to turn the situation around.

As I followed the instructions given by the Holy Spirit, it was revealed to me the reasons why this guy was not the husband God had for me. To honor God required that I trust Him to sever ties without injury and loss. I had to trust Him to provide financially, considering the recent purchase of two homes. Would I compromise the guidance He was providing to play it safe, jeopardizing the long-term plans He had for my life?

I courageously gave the ring back and canceled all plans concerning the marriage. My finances were gravely attacked to the point that I literally had to walk around my house with my eyes closed in worship, confessing to the Father that I chose to walk by faith and not by sight (2 Corinthians 5:7). It was indeed a humbling season of my life, and I recall being in service one Sunday when the pastor asked, "How many here would appreciate any form of a financial blessing right now?" I raised my hand in agreement, and a customer I helped put into their home sitting behind me blessed me with fifty dollars that day. I didn't even have gas money to get through the week of my travel, and the funds received were truly an answer to prayer.

In that season, with my back against the wall, I learned what it meant to trust in the Lord firmly. I experienced deliverance from shopping where I had to choose between paying my basic bills or buying a Michelle outfit.

As I continued to trust the Father through my pains of withdrawals and difficulty, I experienced His signs and wonders. It did not come as I desired them to, but in hindsight, I received what I needed to accelerate my life in the direction of the future that awaited me. It may not be working out the way we planned, but God consistently works all things together for the children who love Him and are called according to the divine purpose and plan He has for them (Romans 8:28).

As I encourage myself in the presence of the Father, the storms subside, the mountains are removed, the peace is felt, my strength is renewed. We put the Father in remembrance of His promises by speaking back to Him His unfailing Word. The Bible says He honors His Word above His name (Psalm 138:2). My life is a testament to speaking the Word in faith and understanding the power of His redemptive love.

Chapter 8

EXECUTION

Maximize your stage

There are people worldwide awaiting their one big shot to be discovered or signed with a professional team to prove themselves worthy of the big stage. As we learn about their journey, we become cheerleaders, hoping for their chance at a life-changing encounter. Their journey required study, practice, and courage. We are inspired by their progress and drawn into their dreams and vision. Every day we awake, we enter our stage called life. We influence the performance of the day, which contributes to the future we desire to have. Based on the vision and levels of success we aim to reach, we discipline ourselves to study, practice, and have the courage to execute.

As a believer, when I commit to studying the Word of God, I gain the understanding of who I am in Christ and embrace the power and authority I possess to impact the world stage. As I meditate on the Word of God and put my understanding into practice, I rise out of the ashes to present on the stage of life my best performance. I begin to believe and embrace that I am a woman fearfully and wonderfully made by God (Psalm 139:14). I acknowledge life's challenges but magnify the God of my salvation by referencing His Word that holds the power to shift outcomes.

I recognize that I am a bearer of His authority in the name of Jesus and formulate my life's stage with every word spoken in faith. I am the head and not the tail, above and not beneath (Deuteronomy 28:13). I am victorious through Christ Jesus (1 Corinthians 15:57). I speak life over my marriage, family, vision, and finances. I acknowledge that the Spirit of the Lord is upon me (Luke 4:18), which helps me produce a stellar performance on my stage daily.

A dormant life spent watching others accomplish success leads to discouragement and self-imposed limitations. It's time to put into practice all you've studied for years. Shake off the doubt and negative self-talk, which produce fear to leave it all out on your stage. Instead, declare, "I can do all things through Christ that strengthens me" (Philippians 4:13).

Through the divine leading of the Holy Spirit, it's time to live your life to the fullest potential and leave it all on the stage, forever impacting the legacy you are to leave on the earth. With your eyes on the Father and your heart receptive to His Word, you can courageously walk on water. You can do the miraculous by the grace of God. The world awaits your greatness.

Chapter 9

COURAGE

Dual release

It's June of 2012, and I stand in the middle of over two hundred guests as the mistress of ceremony for my brother's celebration after graduating from the University of Rhode Island. I've been on my personal journey of healing, restoration, and revelation with the Father through my intimate relationship with the Holy Spirit for the past eleven years. My vision has changed, releasing the compassion to love beyond myself.

For the first time in over thirty years, I saw the family member who impacted my life at eight years old. To my surprise, there was no anger in my heart. Led by the Holy Spirit, I flowed in prayer and engaged the audience. I stood as a testament of grace that comes from the Father, understanding that my decision to forgive and let go honors God and expresses gratitude for all He has forgiven in my life through Christ Jesus, my redeemer (Ephesians 4:32). Everything is a process; the more you choose to walk in obedience even when it doesn't feel good, the more you gain the peace to release.

By the end of the evening, I was approached by that family member. He expressed how proud he was of me and shocked by how I developed as a woman of God. I remember the tears when the Holy Spirit showed me my mom's pains and required that I love her deeply and forgive the hurt that I carried for so many years. I recall the time in the hospital after major surgery when the church friend I thought would be by my side was absent before and after surgery for no reason and, with tears rolling down my face, was led by the Holy Spirit to reach out and let her know I forgave her and held nothing against her. Who am I to doubt the power of the Holy Spirit to transform a person's life considering the work He's done in me? I received his sentiments warmly and continued to greet other guests.

There will be a testing of your faith that challenges what you confess to believe and the new person you proclaim to have become (2 Corinthians 5:17). This process is less about God and more about your preparation for your next level in Him. Can the Father trust you to honor His Word in tough circumstances that may not feel good to your physical and emotional senses?

I learned through experiences the supernatural power working in me. Like in victories throughout the Old Testament in the Bible, forgiveness in unfathomable experiences serves as a monument in my heart of the possibilities in God. Wholehearted forgiveness in my own strength and understanding was impossible, considering the lack of dialogue. What I didn't know at the time was that the battles won in my spirit, soul, and body prepared me for the battles that lay before me. Through my decision to forgive and trust the Holy Spirit, who dwells in me, I, too, received my healing, deliverance, and renewed strength.

The Father knows the end from the beginning, and I'm freed through my decision to forgive the wrongs and afflictions caused by others in my life. I choose to walk in the healing, deliverance, and liberty the Father freely provided.

Receptive to love again

As I grew in my relationship with the Father and intimacy with the Holy Spirit, I understood the importance of working on me. Through previous relationships, "my issues" were revealed and understood through powerful teachings on relationships and marriage. The whole formed in a marriage covenant was only as good as the two individuals joined together.

I recall spending time growing in the Word and my relationship with God and then encountering a young man who was very outgoing, stylish, intelligent, friendly, and we shared a lot in common. We were both community oriented and identified as rising leaders in the area. We had great conversations and good outings together. I recall agreeing to go on a date with him if he would, in turn, agree to come to my church service the following Sunday morning.

Excited and hopeful, I prepared for service the next day, knowing I would be ministering with the dance team. Service was packed with hundreds in attendance at the convention center in Providence. I prayed for a move of God that morning and ministered unto Him with all my heart.

By the end of service, there was an altar call for those who desired to receive salvation by accepting Jesus as Lord of their lives. As the hundreds waited patiently, there was movement from the back, and soon, a male was making his way down the long aisle to the front. It was my guest. I became very emotional and saw then a vision of marrying this man.

I would soon meet his family, and it was love at first sight. His parents adored me, and I gained two younger sisters and a loving young brother. I spent a lot of time with the family, and very soon, this young man expressed giving me an official title in his life. Considering that he had just recently accepted salvation and we both were still learning to walk out that decision, I wanted to take it slow and not move too fast. He received my response as rejection, and things soon began to change. We spent less time together, and we grew apart for a while.

He was sincerely missed, and I remember receiving a call after some time for another outing, and I accepted. We had the most fantastic day together. I would soon fall back into sin while in church and loving God. I found myself in the presence of the Father, crying—devastated by the choices I had made. I found myself in the valley of decision with authority to direct the path of my life deeper into sin or courageously to safety.

With tears running down my face, I made the call and shared the pain of dishonoring my Father. That was the end of the outings and long phone calls, but I still communicated periodically with his family. His mother encouraged me to be hopeful as I watched this young man regularly date and interact with other women. I continued to read books on Christian relationships and attend seminars that challenged me as a woman of God concerning the relationships that honored the Father.

While taking a walk after returning from a Christian conference in Tampa, Florida, with my girlfriend Candy, I was listening to a recording by Dr. Ronn Elmore, and he stated, "Love is not safe," which liberated me that day. After time in the presence of God, I knew that day that I was to courageously share with the young man the desires of my heart and embrace whatever the outcome, for God already knew the end from the beginning and had my best interest at heart. I drafted a thoughtful e-mail that expressed the potential I saw in us exclusively getting to know each other on a deeper level and seeing where God would take the relationship. I also expressed my understanding and appreciation for his consideration of my request, even if he didn't feel the same way. I gave him a call to expect an e-mail from me with the liberty to make a decision he felt best for him.

Within less than thirty minutes, I received a response that this young man was not ready to settle down and wanted to explore his options. The right thing doesn't always feel good, but it is required. I was sad and started playing a DVD from the conference I had just attended in Tampa. It spoke directly to my spirit, and I would worship God with tears running down my face. I felt a release at that moment that I couldn't quite explain. All I wanted was time in the presence of God wrapped in His warm embrace.

Two hours later that same day, I received a call from an unknown out-of-town number. When I picked up, it was Cliff Davidson, a persistent man who received my business card at a wedding in Virginia two months ago that I thought I would never encounter again. He tried to reach me for two months via e-mail and was unaware that I had left my job to honor God with a new business venture. The company finally shut down the e-mail address, and he realized that I possibly didn't receive his messages.

The last time I spoke to Cliff Davidson, I was at the airport on my way home from the wedding, and he was very forward, sharing his heart about wanting to get married and being with a God-fearing woman. The irony here is he had a date at the wedding but indicated they were just friends who both knew the couple. The response from this Brooklyn girl that day was um-hum and ensured I didn't save his number.

It was now two months later, and Cliff wanted just one opportunity to know why I rejected him and never responded to his messages. After having the courage to face the situation with the young man I allowed to endure in my life for over a year, I closed a chapter and made room for God to do something new in my life and bring forth His choice for me. Cliff and I would speak for close to six hours that day, talking as though we had known each other for years. He received my hard truth and understood where I was coming from. It was weeks later, and I still looked forward to our conversations in the midst of a challenging season that stretched me in the formation of a new business. I asked deep questions about his past, present, and desires for the future.

After spending a nice day with him in New York City, I would come home and isolate myself on a three-day fast to hear from God concerning Cliff being the man He had for me. During those three days, He showed me the man Cliff—unedited. He showed me the trials, challenges, and pain we would encounter. By the third day, He confirmed that Cliff Davidson was His choice for me. The tears I shed that day were not tears of joy, but my heart and mind received the will of God, honoring the guidance I've received from the Holy Spirit since I decided to make Jesus Lord of my life, which has brought forth supernatural blessing.

In the garden of Gethsemane, Jesus knew of the cruel affliction He would endure for all mankind and was grieved to the point of death (Matthew 26:36–38). His prayer: "My Father, if it is possible, let this cup pass from Me: yet not as I will, but as You will" (Matthew 26:39). Before ever falling in love with my husband, I fell deeply in love with God, and like a child in the presence of their father, I confidently believed in His love and desire to give me His very best, so I responded to the assignment as my big brother Jesus did and accepted the will of God for my life.

We experienced the trials, challenges, pain, and setbacks but were both made in that process. Cliff Davidson is the absolute best choice for me. Our marriage is bearing much fruit today, which overwhelms me when I think of the faithfulness of God. Anything worth having will require a fight you may not have experienced before. I had to stop fighting with my natural understanding and learn to war in the spirit in the presence of my Father through prayer, thanksgiving, and petition. Love is simply not safe, requiring us to push past the outcomes of yesterday that we may love again.

Courage to pursue

The life-changing doctor's visit that indicated the need for a hysterectomy shook my core. As I sobered up after the longest ten-minute drive of my life, I felt the need for a second opinion. I would see doctors as far as Washington, DC, hoping for a change in prognosis. Appointment after appointment, the responses were vague, making no guarantees yet stating there's always a possibility.

I was prescribed the drug Lupron with the hope of shrinking the massive benign fibroids. The longer I stayed on the medication, the bigger the fibroids grew. I endured menopausal side effects for almost one year while still in my early twenties. I would go to prayer meetings and respond to altar calls for those wanting to be healed from sickness and diseases.

The last altar call I answered related to the struggles with fibroids was in a crowded school auditorium, and the minister had me state my issue through a microphone. The fear that came out of me was intense, thinking of the outcome of my situation. The minister acknowledged my fear and pretty much sent me on my way. It was then I realized that the healing I desired would not come from man but from God.

While watching Christian television, I heard Perry Stone teach from his book *The Meal That Heals*, which taught on the power of Jesus's crucifixion and resurrection represented through communion. As I read the book, the power of faith came over me and would begin my daily communion, expecting God's healing power to deliver me. I'm now at the halfway point of the second year dealing with this infirmity. I would take communion daily for six months, confessing the Word of God and expecting His blessed assurance over my life.

The doctor's report began to shift, and very soon, the need for hysterectomy was not required, but there would be a procedure. I was so confident in the power of the resurrection working in my life that I began to share possible names of my future children. Those who knew my struggles were very uncomfortable.

After the procedure, the doctors were dumbfounded by the fibroid growth they discovered in my body, yet I was extremely healthy. A procedure that should have taken approximately two hours lasted seven hours, requiring a blood transfusion. In the midst of it all, I worshipped the Father and firmly believed his report concerning me. The doctor would enter the room once I was awake to warn me of the need to have a child within the next twelve months before that door closes for me based on what he had experienced through the surgery.

Fear and anxiety can lead to impulsive actions resulting in poor outcomes. I calmly looked the doctor in the eye and acknowledged he was heard. My Father instructed the need to be anxious for nothing, but in all things, through prayer and supplication, with thanksgiving to let my request be known unto Him (Phil 4:6). I was single and had not met my husband at the time. To attempt to have a child within twelve months would require taking things into my own hands. Instead, I would hold on to the concession of my faith and wait two years to be married. Right after marriage, a family friend who watched my tough health journey approached me with the question: "So when will you have children?"

Without a doubt, I responded, "this time next year, I will be holding my child."

My Father did not let my confession of faith fall to the ground and blessed our union with the birth of our son Jeremiah twelve months later.

What is that deep desire given to you by God that is being threatened by the experiences of your life? How big have you made God in your life? Is He only able to provide you with employment, a roof over your head, and clothes on your back? The Word of God tells me in Luke 1:37 that nothing shall be impossible with Him. In this chapter of Luke, we read about a virgin woman, Mary, who would receive a divine visitation from an angel named Gabriel, who revealed to her the favor to be impregnated with the Savior of the world, who is the son of God to be named Jesus. In verse 38, Mary responds, "May it be done to me according to your word."

It was also in this same chapter that the priest Zacharias and his wife, Elizabeth, both righteous in the sight of God, would be delivered from barrenness through the petitions made to the Lord for a child in their old age (Luke 1:13). God responds to faith that brings forth supernatural blessings amid impossible odds. Each breakthrough experienced strengthens your faith to go deeper in your walk with God.

I was content with the birth of Jeremiah, but my husband also desired a daughter. When I began to exercise my faith in God to bring life again out of my wound, I experienced attacks but held on to the promise and assurance of His faithfulness. In the fifth year of marriage, our miracle twins Destiny Grace and Danielle Joy were born. God will give you double for faith exercised in the midst of trouble. Courageously pursue the desires of your heart aligned with the Word of God.

Chapter 10

DIVINELY QUALIFIED AND APPOINTED

Divinely qualified

My life used to be such that when I assessed myself, I didn't feel worthy of the vision that God had given me. I didn't feel worthy to be on the platforms He showed me; I was paralyzed with fear. Could I dare to dream those types of dreams and see myself on that level? Who am I? A young woman who met her daddy in her twenties for the first time. A young girl who fell prey to the slick talk of a boy and would lose what was most sacred to her by the time she was a teenager. A girl who, by her early teens, was frequenting nightclubs and dating guys way older than her.

Who am I to see myself on that level? I ran like Jonah from destiny, from purpose, from the call of God on my life (Jonah 1:2–3). I chose to play it safe, but I found myself in the belly of a whale (Jonah 1:17). I found myself in a dark place that only God could get me out of. It was in that place that I went deeper with the Father and received the guidance and support of the Holy Spirit. With great uncertainty, I chose to walk in the things He had called me to, rejecting that spirit of fear that always tries to lift its head in so many areas of my life.

I often encountered women who appeared healthy, strong, and whole yet can see past their facade revealing the condition of their soul. I've walked in their shoes and many of their experiences, which afforded me the capacity to understand their thoughts, struggles, and pain. The deliverance I've experienced in life was not just for me and my household. There are lives awaiting my obedience to experience divine liberation through the hearing of my testimony and process of healing.

It was my sister-friend Kim, through years of hearing me share my journey, who began to encourage me to share my story with other women. There is a ministry in each of us to stand as a bridge and bring daughters back to the presence of their heavenly Father so that they may experience His divine healing and abundance. Promotion and the divine assignment come from the Lord. Understand today, if it's spoken by God concerning you, you are divinely qualified to maximize the vision.

Will of the Father

Have you ever been busy with your day, consumed, working hard, doing so many things to touch the lives of people that the world would consider a good thing? You know you are a good person, very giving, invested in the lives of others, invested in church, invested at work but yet feeling so unfulfilled, feeling a void and lost. That comes when you're out of the will of God, busy but yet not called or walking in your anointing and divine purpose. I've been there—working hard, pleasing the pastors, pleasing the church but dying because what I was doing was church, and what God was calling me to was kingdom. God was calling me to a life fulfilled in Him, operating in the purpose and the giftings that He had called me to. It may have taken me out of my element and required that I walk in courage and uncertainty, but it would lead me to a place of fulfillment.

Fulfillment comes in the presence of the Father, aligning you with His perfect will for your life. So as a woman still learning to become who God had already created me to be, I found myself going down so many paths yet lacking His joy, peace, anointing, and His grace to execute what was before me on a high level.

It wasn't until I got to a place of walking not in my own understanding but rather knowing I was obeying the instructions of God that I began to experience what we now know as breakthrough in my household. Not fully understanding my experiences, I had to go through my journey to be developed in my process to get to a place of obedience that I can say to God, "With You, 'everything is possible'" (Matthew 19:26).

Father God, I know that sometimes, it just seems like I'm getting nowhere, but it could be that I'm not operating in alignment with Your will, plan, and purpose for my life. So today, I choose to lay down Michelle. I choose to lay down her will, her physical abilities and take on the supernatural that comes when the greater that is in me is glorified in the world (1 John 4:4).

When I take on the desires of God, which ultimately leads me to the place of joy and happiness, I receive the fulfillment that I'm desiring in my life. I received that next level. I received that peace that surpasses all understanding, joy that is everlasting, that comes in His presence (Philippians 4:7). It comes on His frequency. I had to learn that thought process. I had to learn it the hard way, fighting and resisting my next level.

I pray as you are reading the words in this book today that you choose to surrender to the perfect will of the Father for your life (Romans 12:2).

I surrender… I surrender to trying to do this thing in my own strength, allowing the world to define who I am to be. Lord, I'm asking the question of You today: what would You have me be? What would You have me do? I want to fulfill that purpose. I want to seek after that, knowing You know what's best for me. Before I ever called, You had already answered me (Isaiah 65:24). Knowing in that place with You is fullness of joy, peace, strength, and acceleration to the glory of Your Name. Hallelujah! I want that more than I want anything else. So help me, Lord, through this process to get there.

His grace is sufficient

If the vision doesn't scare you, it's not God. Nothing He assigns us to do will be possible solely in our own strength. We, as the children of God, through our decision to be saved, are carriers of a supernatural anointing that brings light to dark places and hope to the lost (Isaiah 61:1–3). The Father sees the heart and does not appoint based on the world's standards, giving everyone the opportunity to be an instrument of His glory.

In the book of Judges, chapter 6, the children of Israel were severely oppressed by their enemies due to the evil decisions they made in life. Their struggles were so harsh that they had to make homes in caves and mountains, growing only crops sustainable in that climate. The magnitude of pain in their circumstances was so intense that they cried out to God for help against their enemies (Judges 6:6). It was Gideon whom the angel of the Lord visited and to whom proclaimed, "The Lord is with you, O valiant warrior" (Judges 6:12), to be an answer to the cries of the people and deliverance for a nation. Gideon reminded the angel that his family was the least of the Manasseh tribe and that he happened to be the youngest of his father's house (Judges 6:16). When the Father gives the assignment and we push past fear to obediently honor His will, we accomplish the supernatural.

We are awaiting the crowds and the qualified to show up and execute what the Father has instructed us to do because we still struggle with poor self-image and operate through the lens of fear. Yes, it's natural to doubt and feel insecurities, but the Bible states in 1 John 4:4 that we, the children of God, have overcome those strongholds in our mind and physical environment that are hindering our progression in life, for greater is the Holy Spirit of God that is in us than anything that will ever come against us in this world.

As Gideon learned in Judges 7, with God, you do not need the huge multitudes of people to win in life. He's aligning you with individuals with the right mindset, developed character, and reverence of the Father to not only win the battle faced but to sustain a victorious life. Although there were twenty-two thousand who started out with Gideon to face the adversaries robbing them of their peace, that actual army he led into battle was only three hundred men. You—a person firmly committed to honoring the Father in your life, pushing past your own understanding, customs, and status quo—will become the dominant majority in every situation in life.

My constant prayer was for God to help my unbelief that my spiritual eyes would be opened to see that as a redeemed woman, through the saving grace of Jesus, there is always more with me than are against me (2 Kings 6:17). Michelle does not possess the power in her own strength to overcome generational deficiencies, poverty, negative self-image, oppression, and setback. Through the love of God and redemption through the resurrection of Christ Jesus, I've learned that even with some natural uncertainty, I can do all things through Christ who strengthens me (Philippians 4:13).

Like I and Gideon in Judges 6:25, God requires us to remove the altars we have built in our lives that are contrary to His will, serving as a barrier to breaking down the strongholds hindering the experience of a life we desire. Similar to Gideon, the Father knows just where we are. It is up to us to acknowledge the need for His help and always inquire of the Holy Spirit to guide our path. In that place, we experience the sufficiency of His grace and supernatural power that encompasses us in our most vulnerable state (2 Corinthians 12:9). In all I have experienced in life, I've seen time and time again the sufficiency of His grace, infallible victory realized in a life surrendered to His will.

Trinity mortgage solutions

The more my intimacy grew with the Father, the more I would have visions of my future that intimidated me. My heart to serve others, primarily in the area of empowerment, kept me active in local organizations, community events, churches, amongst family and friends. I believe that we all have the potential to be great with the proper support along the way.

At the age of twenty-three, I was recruited and hired by the vice president of mortgage operations at a major bank in the area to improve their mortgage lending pull through amongst people of color. That manager, John, would become a great mentor in my life and exposed me to opportunities and training that transformed my possibilities. It was through that experience that I understood the importance of taking ownership of my career and managing the opportunity as an entrepreneur to build my brand and clientele.

My approach was simply treating community members with the respect they deserved while providing the knowledge and available resources needed for a down payment in securing a home. Within two years, the once underserved communities became the most productive book of business for the mortgage lending department and catapulted me to the number one mortgage loan officer for my employer in the state of Rhode Island.

As the Lord prepares you for your next level, He will expose you to opportunities to prepare for what lies ahead. I was extremely comfortable in my position while helping to improve the lives of many families. Soon the bank would outsource their mortgage department and lose sight of the importance of customer service. My manager would leave the organization, and I would follow suit twelve months later.

I worked for another well-established lender for a couple of years and was then preparing to take a big leap of faith by opening my own mortgage company at the age of twenty-eight. I was literally shaking in my knees but knew I heard from my Father to move forward. I was the only managing member of the organization, and I compiled an advisory team with the expertise to provide guidance along the way. Justin, Simon, and Karriem were vested members of that advisory team, and firmly supported along the way. I would hire a strong team that represented the communities we served and began to push forward guided by the principles found in the Word of God.

My faith was truly stretched at the initial stages of the launch, but we grew and were well positioned to move into our own establishment after only twelve months of operation. We never experience the power of divine grace operating in only what's familiar and comfortable. In hindsight, I also understand wholeheartedly the power released when the decision is made to honor the Father by obediently moving in faith as He provides direction.

Chapter 11

THE FIRE REQUIRED

As a mother, it is my natural instinct to nurture, preserve, and protect. I overcame so much to finally be pregnant with a child of my own. I recall struggling to pick names, and the name Jeremiah was suggested for our son. I would go to the book of Jeremiah, and after reading the first chapter, I felt the presence of God and a foreshadow of the legacy of my bloodline.

The name Jeremiah, in Hebrew, means "Yahweh (God) will exalt." I cried, feeling a great call on the life of our son but not understanding then the road he would travel as God prepares him for the platforms He's called him to. As Cliff and I prayed for Jeremiah, I was regularly led to prophesy on his impact on the world and his generation.

By the time Jeremiah was three, he would practice his sermons with his little sisters, and by six and seven, he prophesied accurately into the lives of his father and me that left us astounded by his gifts. At seven, he and I attended a water baptism for adults from our church looking to publicly profess their faith and new life in Christ. Jeremiah went to the front of the church, and there was a big Bible profiled to the left that he desired to read. He would then come back to me and state that today was his day to be publicly baptized. I tried to explain the process and agreed to enroll him in the next baptism class. He was adamant that today was his day.

As we sat down to commence the service, Pastor Rudy declared that there was someone here also ready to be baptized. Jeremiah bounced out of his chair and raised his hand. At that moment, I realized the need to let go and let God do in the son He entrusted to Cliff and me what He desired to do. I called Cliff quickly and asked that He bring him a change of clothes and a towel. At the precious age of seven, Jeremiah stood confidently with a mic in his hands and eloquently expressed His relationship with the Father and desire to live for Him.

Very soon after that, there was a declaration of war against the life of our son to the point, we couldn't recognize the brave, bold, expressive, intelligent leader we had grown to love. In the book of Isaiah, chapter 43, verse 2, the Word of the Lord states, "When you pass through the waters, I will be with you; and through the rivers, they shall not overflow you. When you walk through the fire, you shall not be burned, nor shall the flame scorch you."

Jeremiah went from leading school programs and closing the talent show to coming home and asking if he is really that ugly? He was now a victim of bullying on a daily basis and experienced trials designed to break his confidence and silence his voice. His engagement is now at an ultimate low, and although I'm actively communicating with teachers and administration, things are not improving.

After many sleepless nights and time in prayer, I had to allow God to do in this situation what He desired to do. As a mother, I wanted to take my son out of the toxic environment he was experiencing, but God had a greater purpose.

For the next four years, I was immersed in the state of education in urban communities. I would regularly testify at the statehouse, serve on boards, and contribute to the state's Every Student Succeeds Act (ESSA) to help ensure a better educational experience for many underserved youths coming from similar communities like mine.

At my son's school, I made the charter organization the focus of my capstone master's project with the goal of shedding some light on the changes necessary to appropriately support children of color.

It was through that process and the many experiences of my son that I understood the assignment at that charter network. Like Abraham in the book of Genesis, chapter 22, we are all faced with testing that will expose the condition of our heart and our commitment to the covenant we have with the Father. Jeremiah, my only son, whom I had labored in prayer for years even prior to being married, was being destroyed in an environment that we had the means to remove him from. Allowing Jeremiah to stay in that environment while praying him through the struggles and challenges was our sacrifice to God since the greater purpose was to expose the systemic racism embedded in that charter network negatively impacting the lives of so many families.

As the hard questions were asked of leadership and the local board of the organization, policies began to shift, and people were removed. Jeremiah and some of the other scholars pushed past concerns of retaliation to share their candid experiences with the board governing the charter network here in Rhode Island. With the recent rise of social consciousness related to racism and oppression sparked by violence resulting in the premature death of African Americans, the seed God used the Davidson family to plant will bear fruit. The storms and fire faced by Jeremiah and the entire family did not have the power to kill us; instead, it strengthened our voice for the work that lies ahead.

Without the fire experienced, I am not sure the character and fortitude that I see in our son today would have been developed. It has strengthened his faith and confidence in the God who created him. He transitioned out of the charter network into a new environment for seventh grade, but we're grateful to have supported the families left behind by sowing into a better future for their children.

Embrace the fire that God leads you to. You are refined in His presence for the life He desires you to experience. ***STORMS WILL COME AGAINST THOSE THAT YOU LOVE. BUT IF YOU ALLOW GOD TO BE THE CAPTAIN OF THE SHIP, THE STORMS WILL BE USED FOR HIS GLORY... FOR ALL THINGS WORK TOGETHER FOR THE GOOD OF THOSE***

THAT LOVE HIM AND CALLED ACCORDING TO HIS DIVINE PURPOSE.

As you push forward, expect opposition, understanding that the weapons formed against you do not have the ability to prosper as a child of God (Isaiah 54:17). The more I stood on the Word in the midst of storms, learning to maintain my peace, the more I experienced the hand of God moving on my behalf. It is not our responsibility to fight for ourselves (2 Chronicles 20:15). Every major victory experienced will come in a posture of worship and praise, declaring to the Father, "I trust you in all things" (2 Chronicles 20:21–22 AMP). He will never fail the one who chooses to put Him in His rightful place and believe the promises spoken through His Word.

Fail forward

If I continue to limit myself because of what I don't know, don't quite understand, but yet there is a calling on my life, something to pursue, I will never learn through the experiences before me the areas that I need to grow and address. I will never learn what it means to step out of the boat and at least attempt to walk on water. I will never know what it means to live courageously.

At the age of twenty-eight years old, a young woman who grew up in tough housing communities as a child, displaced from one home to the next, slept in living rooms, slept on floors: a young woman whose mother did the best she could yet stayed in apartments with no electricity and had to be very innovative to survive through imaginary candlelight dinners and camping trips, using the heat of the oven to keep warm, opened a mortgage company to empower the communities she served. No business partners but, with the help of some friends in the industry, received the guidance required to get started to accomplish what she never dreamt was possible. God will give you dreams that will scare you since it was never meant for you to accomplish on your own. The Holy Spirit was that mentor, guide, and friend who I could regularly inquire and would lead me to the people and resources to pursue in order to get the needs met.

Within the first three months of operation, my company grossed over six figures, and I hired a team to move the business forward. By month 11, through the guidance of the Holy Spirit, I purchased the building occupying the business and was having great success. By 2008, we experienced the impact of the financial crisis and had to adjust our business model as we pushed through the storm. In the midst of this external storm, I'm carrying my first child whom I've labored in prayer for while dealing with the tremendous challenges facing a young marriage.

By 2010, while still evolving to keep the business afloat, I learned I was now pregnant with twins, and soon after, my husband began to experience pains in his chest while playing basketball. After one week of constant pain, I woke up with an urgency for my husband to go to the hospital. Being pregnant and having our two-year-old son in the back seat, I left him at the door of the hospital and asked that he give me a call once he received his checkup.

Hours went by, and Cliff wasn't answering the phone. I decided to go back to the hospital to inquire about his status. My husband had been moved to ICU because for the past week, blood was oozing throughout his body since the valve to his heart had come apart. He was admitted immediately to the hospital indefinitely. It was just thirty days before my husband was laid off due to the impact of the financial crisis, and we no longer had medical insurance as he awaited the start of a new job.

FATHER, really? Father, You have brought me a mighty long way, and through it all, You have been faithful. You have tremendous confidence in me and will never allow me to experience more than I can bear (1 Corinthians 10:13). Father, I choose to maintain my peace during the storm. Holy Spirit, I thank You for Your love and guidance that will ensure victory amid this storm. Father, You would not bless me with children and leave them fatherless. I choose to trust You and lean not on my natural understanding, knowing even now, You are directing our path to safety (Proverbs 3:5–6).

For the months to come, my belly would grow exponentially to the point that I was asked regularly if I was having twins while going back and forth to support my husband in the hospital and maintain the business. My peace and countenance were baffling to the doctors caring for my husband, considering my physical condition. His peace is greater than our circumstances and developed through relationship and intimacy (Philippians 4:7). Through all the health challenges, we were facing tremendous financial difficulty that, considering all we're encountering, would have been easy to pin all on the devil. We tend to lack ownership of our outcomes, empowering external forces like the devil as having the power to bring destruction over our lives.

In my quiet place with the Holy Spirit, He showed me how I missed His shift to financial safety. He was redirecting me and showed me the instructions and guidance needed through the people He brought my way to change our course for a financial breakdown but was consumed by the brand created as the "mortgage lady."

See, in 2007, there was a women's conference established, and I had the honor of pouring into over two hundred women in attendance. I would encounter women I wasn't aware were in the room, and they would close the door and share the impact of my testimony on their lives and the healing of broken relationships. I was often invited to speak at events and would politely decline because I was too busy with my mortgage business. The Father wasn't surprised by the financial crisis of 2008 and desired to preserve me from some of the challenges I experienced. I had not reached a point in my development with my friend the Holy Spirit to firmly adhere to HIS guidance and wisdom, grateful that HIS mercy is made new daily in the lives of his people (Lamentations 3:22–23) and willing to receive our heartfelt repentance and redirect our path.

I learned hands-on the resolve, resilience, perseverance, courage, compassion, love, and focus required to overcome in life. No book or conversation could have assimilated the experiences faced during that time. There are some things you must go through to make you. The outcomes may not always be what you desire, but the Father knows the road that you have taken and the destination that lies ahead. If we allow the Holy Spirit to light the path, we are led to safety.

Although the circumstances were challenging and I experienced loss, it did not have the power to destroy me. Instead, it catapulted me to my next level. My faith and trust in the Father through the leading of the Holy Spirit grew from that process. There were many who lost everything, yet I found myself still married with healthy children, owner of commercial real estate (although that business later closed), and a certified Christian life coach developing conferences and events to enrich the lives of God's daughters.

As the economy recovered, the experience gained as a mortgage broker opened tremendous doors to represent national lenders in a management role in my respective market. I would use that platform to stand as a testament to the possibilities in God while impacting more lives around economic empowerment. The commercial building became the location of my mother's restaurant, where she shared her culinary gifts with the world, nourishing and strengthening her community. We have since passed on the knowledge and experience gained to a family restaurant at that location, continuing to serve the community. God knows the end from the beginning (Isaiah 46:10). The experience gained through failure was my greatest teacher.

Position, not identity

I have painfully watched gifted and anointed people blessed with great influence and promise accelerate from a place of obscurity, who then abuse their platform, lifting God's anointing from their lives and requiring them to hold on to the titles given by man as their qualification. In the book of 1 Samuel, chapters 9–10, Samuel, God's appointed leader and prophet, was instructed to anoint as the king of Israel, Saul, a man from the lineage of Benjamin. Not only was this the smallest of the Israelite tribes, but Saul was also from a family identified as the least in his community at the time.

It is natural and truthful to feel unqualified for the positions that God graciously calls us to. When the posture of our heart remains intimate and dependent on the God who has brought forth the position and elevation, we continue to be consistently successful. As a newly appointed king, Saul followed the guidance of God and the mentorship of His leader Samuel. He experienced the Spirit of God, who gave him divine instructions and favor to destroy the enemies coming against the nation he was now appointed to lead.

In chapter 13 of 1 Samuel, the actions of Saul angered his enemies, and they assembled in great multitudes to destroy Israel. Although Saul was aware of the instructions of God and the role Samuel played in securing their victory, he allowed his insecurities as a leader and the opinions deriving from fear inspired by others to take things into his own hands as the king of Israel. Saul dishonored God but expected, based on his position as king, to receive the same favor he was accustomed to in bringing forth defeat over his enemies. Samuel then declared to Saul,

> But now your kingdom shall not endure.
> The Lord has sought out for Himself a man after
> His own heart, and the Lord has appointed him
> as ruler over His people because you have not
> kept what the Lord commanded you. (verse 14)

I have failed God over and over again, even when desiring to do the right things. I can never be good or perfect enough to honor God. Jesus, who knew no sin, bore my sins and that of every person who receives Him as Lord, becoming righteous through His name while striving to live a life that brings honor to God (2 Corinthians 5:21).

Can I get to a place of divine dependency, understanding His counsel and guidance bring forth the assurance needed in life to succeed on every level? It requires a shift in thinking that challenges processes accepted as the standard. Gaining revelation and understanding yet unapplied results in a defeated life. I must reassess my perception of success guiding the actions I take.

Various circumstances challenge our position and aspirations, and when we take things into our own hands, it can lead to spiritual death while still in our current position. Our titles remain the same, and we may not see the harm done spiritually to the future that lies ahead. As a young CEO in my late twenties, I had the right intentions but truly did not know how to lead others with the heart of

God. I found myself emulating the actions of other leaders based on the success I perceived. I was soon the leader of none, struggling to hold the pieces together and keep the ship from sinking.

My identity had to be realigned with my Creator and Father, who established the open doors before me that I may have the capacity to maximize the position, understanding that it was only by His grace that I am what I am and choosing to courageously honor the access and platforms He has provided (1 Corinthians 15:10). I am grateful for the mercy of my Father made new in the life of believers each day, not withholding His faithfulness (Lamentations 3:23). I do not want to live a life absent from the presence of God with His glory departed.

We can hold on to our positions as spouses, parents, business owners, government officials, community leaders, educators, pastors, prophets, evangelists, and Christians without the anointing of God that breaks the yokes that produce supernatural signs and wonders. The progress we desire in our respective positions is birthed in the presence of God, where our identity as children made in His image and likeness is affirmed. It is through that posture that we fall in love with our Creator, desiring to honor Him with our lives and positions that we experience His holistic success. By the grace of God and the divine guidance of the Holy Spirit, our marriage, children, and businesses can be overwhelmingly blessed. I want to be right with God.

Chapter 12

SURRENDER TO YOUR PROCESS

Prepare to soar

Olympians have one shot every four years to compete on the largest international stage, showcasing their tireless preparation to be crowned the best of their respective sport. Not everyone is presented with this opportunity every four years, and there's always the risk of injury derailing the preparation to compete.

Is life much different? We are all given free will to improve our giftings, pursue aspirations, develop disciplines, and sharpen our character and development to appropriately position ourselves for the opportunities desired. There are many overlooked with the potential to be successful due to not meeting the requirements for promotion.

I have remorsefully witnessed some of the most gifted young athletes in my community drop out of school, end up in prison, or become parents at young ages, changing the course of their future. For years, I would talk about the greatness I witnessed in their lives but unfortunately harmed by external pressures. It was always my prayer that although they did not excel based on the expectations birthed through their giftings, their lives would experience a positive change of course.

Everything worth having will require preparation and discipline to go where we haven't gone before and do what hasn't yet been accomplished through perseverance. As individuals prepare to climb high altitudes, they are warned to stay hydrated, avoid drinking alcohol during travel, and stay low to allow their body time to acclimatize. When a believer prepares to go to greater heights in God, time is spent postured low, minimizing interactions with others to dedicate consistent time in prayer and fasting, consuming high consumptions of water, and eliminating toxic consumption of alcohol that dehydrates and impairs cognitive reasoning.

The old life and irrational decisions will destroy you on higher levels. Although I didn't drink alcohol, there were flaws in my character and reasoning that I had to release to be afforded the opportunity to go higher and soar in my development. God is no respecter of persons (Romans 2:11), showing no favoritism or partiality amongst His children. He doesn't promote based on your length of time in church or other individuals' opinion of who is deserving. Instead, He examines the heart, our desire to repent, development in His presence, and desire to do His will.

Can I rejoice with that sister blessed with the thing I'm also believing God for knowing that if He did it for her, He can do it for me? Can I stop being wise in my own eyes, doing and associating with the things I desire although I know consciously are wrong? Can I extend forgiveness to those who have sincerely wounded me, leaving the offense to God to fight for me? Can I take that tough step to improve my skills by enrolling in training or acquiring the formal education necessary for my next level?

The Father doesn't give us more than we can handle, which includes promotion and elevation we are not prepared for. In that low place in the presence of the Father, we gain new strength, developing our ability to sustainably soar in confidence and reach altitudes only dreamt possible (Isaiah 40:31).

Change is complex, considering its opposition to the reasoning we've held on to for years. If our understanding becomes the ultimate factor guiding our decisions, we continue to struggle even though we're praying. I stayed on the same level for years, holding on to what I knew. I see now the years it took for me to embrace the change required to climb to higher altitudes. The Father was patient, receiving my cries for forgiveness, wanting to break free from the strongholds that had me bound. It was in that place that I discovered the liberty received when I keep my eyes on the Father and allow His Word to bring forth instructions that strengthen me for the journey ahead (Psalm 121:1–2). Transformation should be the byproduct of time spent in the presence of God.

Aptitude for the altitude

I gave my life to Christ and found myself in the presence of God, continuously reminiscing on my past. I remembered my pain and experiences. I found myself regularly asking these questions: Father, why did I have to go through this? Why, at the age of five or six, I had to carry myself as an adult, be so wise and intelligent at a young age to survive, had to push myself to handle things that children twice my age didn't have to experience. Father, why was I robbed of my childhood? Why did I have to experience the pains I did? Why did I have to go through the hurt? Why did I have to feel the infliction of the wounds that I did growing up?

It was in the presence of God that He began, through the years of my walk with Him, to show me through the testing, trials, and pain the development that took place in me, the person. He showed me the giftings, skill set, courage, compassion, and leadership produced in me. He showed me the love, understanding, and wisdom that I gained, not just from what I heard but what I experienced. He showed me the compassion I grew for others to love my neighbor as myself. He showed me how to love deeper than I ever thought imaginable so I could be able to experience kingdom love, a love that came from God, to be able to embrace it on a high level.

That was only possible through the pain endured through my personal journey. It made it possible to see life from the lens of my mother. I felt her pain and gained the perspective of her understanding in order to love her as I do today. It was through that marriage that I said, "God, I did the things on paper that I was to do to be successful, but yet I'm struggling and want to give up." It was in that place that I was made. It was through those experiences I could sift the advice from leaders and stand today happily married. I had to experience those things to relevantly speak to the lives of others and help bring forth deliverance. It was through that financial business that I, a woman in my midtwenties, took on, although I had no one before me that walked that path.

But yet God was calling me to this level and had to face fear and do it anyway. I had to do it, knowing that there was a lot I didn't understand, knowing I had challenges and areas of lack and gap, but yet God said move. I had to learn to obediently move on a high level, move to the point there was no true intellectual assessment of loss. Since I left my job and I owned a home, I had to trust that God would provide. He will make a way, He will give provision, He will accelerate. I had to walk it out. I couldn't just talk about it. I had to walk it out. I had to experience it because God was preparing me for the places He was taking me. He was preparing me for the levels and heights, for the altitude that He desired for me to fly.

It wasn't through what I read and heard; it was through what I experienced and gained through my survival. I gained the resilience and resolve to be the woman that I am today, a woman submitted to the fact that if God is for me, who or what can be against me and win (Romans 8:31)? I understand today that everything I've been through served a purpose for the places, the heights, the people, the interactions that God was preparing to take me to. I understand today that my deliverance wasn't just about Michelle Davidson, my marriage, my children. It was about a nation, my country of Liberia, West Africa, and women in African countries, my sisters here in the US and all over the world that would hear about this story, my journey, and relate to my pain and struggle.

They, too, have asked the questions, God, why did I go through these experiences? Why did I hurt? Understand today that God does not give us more than we can handle. Instead, as we run to the Father with our arms wide open, willing and able to receive Him in the fullness of all that He has for us, we realize that if it had not been for the things we endured, the woman, wife, mother, leader, business person, and the Michelle that I am today wouldn't be possible. So, Father God, thank you for orchestrating my life and doing in me what was only possible in your presence.

As I think about my journey, I think about Queen Esther (book of Esther). I think about her journey. I think of her being an orphan. I think about the pains of not having her parents and being exiled in a foreign land. Yet you sent her a guardian. You sent her Mordecai, her cousin, one who would give her tough love, the one who would provide guidance and instruction. Instructions didn't always feel good with uncertainty, I'm sure, but she obeyed, knowing that Mordecai cared for her, loved her, and wanted the best for her. You did that for me, Lord, through the Holy Spirit. You came as my guide. You have been my keeper and guide through the experiences of life that through my process, like Queen Esther, I, too, would prepare to maximize my position in the kingdom.

Queen Esther was in a foreign kingdom and prepared for twelve months to meet the king (Esther 2:12). The Bible says that her beauty impressed everyone who saw her, and she was selected to be queen. I know today through revelation that what they saw when they laid eyes on Esther wasn't just physical beauty. It was the anointing. It was the grace of God that is upon the lives of His daughters. That grace that is upon the lives of His people causes us in the crowd of millions to be selected, to be favored in the name of Jesus. For Esther, her position was greater than the title of being named queen. As queen, her position was preparing her for a greater purpose found in the presence of God. Our divine position is revealed in prayer as we seek the will of the Father for our lives.

Father, I thank You that You tend to orchestrate all things for our good. You already knew the plans that the enemy had to destroy us, but You had already raised a standard against him. You have already put things in motion, but the question remains, who is that son or daughter willing to move in their rightful position through the courage to seek Your face, fast, and embrace the assignment to face that trial that seems impossible? It defies natural understanding and defies protocol. Who is that son or daughter who will answer that high call, that call from the Father? Queen Esther sought Your face, along with the Jewish people, to receive divine guidance, strategy, favor, and wisdom that comes only from You.

Esther courageously prepared to go see an earthly king to execute the divine assignment established even before her birth to save and set free God's people. Her courage and wisdom were developed in the presence of the Lord that she may soar to altitudes and levels never dreamt possible as an orphan. Father, it was through her obedience and willingness to receive tough love and challenging teachings that You used Mordecai to position her for destiny. The Holy Spirit is preparing my life and the lives of Your daughters to impact nations, reconcile Your people back to You, and receive Your elevation.

It was in that place that Queen Esther's father figure, Mordecai, was blessed. He was blessed and placed into his rightful place of authority (Esther 8:2). The breakthrough of others is connected to your obedience. Like Queen Esther, Mordecai was honored because he compassionately loved God and his people and courageously obeyed the instructions received through prayer. God looks at the heart of man.

Father, You look at the conditions of our heart and our love for one another. You are the one who promotes. Promotion doesn't come from the north, south, east, or west; promotion comes from the Lord, who made heaven and the earth (Psalm 75:6). It was through Your promotion that Mordecai gained authority in a foreign land, and Your daughter Esther was positioned on the throne as queen.

Father, I thank You that today, I no longer cry about what I've been through starting from my childhood. I no longer cry about all I've endured. Instead, I thank You that through that process, You were with me. Before I ever knew You, You knew me, Lord—hallelujah—and prepared me to walk in the presence of kings, to experience my lifting, and speak to the hearts of my sisters all over this world that my testimony would help catapult them to a greater level of freedom and liberty found in You. You prepared for me a table in the presence of my enemies (Psalm 23:5). You prepared me to shine brightly in the midst of trials, for the battle is not mine to fight; the battle is and will continuously be the Lord's (2 Chronicles 20:15).

Father, I understand now, to fly at the altitudes that You are calling me to had nothing to do with whether or not I felt as though I was fully prepared and equipped. It had all to do with following Your instructions and operating in a high level of obedience. I gain understanding through the Word of God, through teachings, through education for the places that You are desiring me to go. I understand today that Your anointing is the distinguishing factor that illuminates giftings. It reveals to the woman or man walking in obedience to Your high call even when they don't understand and are afraid yet trusting that the God who started the good work is faithful to perfect and complete it (Philippians 1:6).

I choose, like Queen Esther and Mordecai, to be an instrument of Your glory. I choose to fly at altitudes that make me feel uncomfortable, knowing that through everything I've been through, You have equipped me with the aptitude to fly on these levels. You have been preparing me for such a time. You have prepared my life, and so many sisters, as a voice to this generation. Today, You are honored. You are glorified. As we testify of the goodness of our Lord, Savior, waymaker, Redeemer, friend, protector, and guardian, we declare that all glory belongs to You.

When Your people are led by the Holy Spirit, we receive the guidance that ensures nothing is missing, broken, or lacking in our lives. Instead, You would restore the years that the cankerworm has stolen (Joel 2:25). Everything that Queen Esther lost as a child, You multiplied in her walk and obedience with You. Everything I experienced as a child that bought me grief and pain is now standing as the testament of joy found in You.

My relationship with my mother is now more than I could ever ask for. During the years of trials, when the business was failing and things were falling apart in my home, she was always there. She never missed a day. She never stopped praying, crying out for my deliverance, healing, and provision. She is the one who sits with me today and, by the grace of God, enjoys the fruit of my life. She is the one today who enjoys the release of God's glory in our lives. She receives love and compassion from her grandchildren and gratitude from her children. She is the one who has the provision to live well and not worry about tomorrow. She is the one whom God used mightily in my life.

At one time, I wanted to curse her; now, all I want to do is bless her. All I want to do is thank her for her sacrifice, for her example as a woman of resilience, a hard worker who pursued vision and mission with all diligence to see the faithfulness of God manifested in her life. She was my walking example of what was possible. Even when I didn't understand or know You as Lord and Savior of my life, You used my mother's journey and resolved to train me for the wars that I would face, to train my hands and give me hinds' feet that I would be able to climb the roughest mountains that were before me.

You used my mother and past as part of my preparation for the palace. Today, I glorify Your name. I rejoice, knowing that although I would not want to experience my past again, the Michelle who is before the world today would not exist if it weren't for that journey. So, Father, I thank You that You definitely know what's best for me. I thank You for the life that was orchestrated in Your presence. I thank You for the healing, for the preparation to soar on the altitudes that You were calling me to in this season of my life.

My children are watching, and my husband is embracing the journey with me, and we're supporting each other as we soar to heights perceived impossible based on how our marriage began. But You, God, know best. We are continuously soaring and developing in Your presence. We now have the fortitude to do so because of all we've endured.

Chapter 13

EMBRACE HIM AS LORD

Created for this

The day I arrive, assuming that I've become all I've been created to be, is the day I begin to die spiritually. We never arrive, understanding each day, I have the opportunity to grow from experiences that sharpen me, the person to execute the ministries God has entrusted in my care. As I improve, my marriage is fruitful, my children are blessed, my professional work is favored, church and blood family are strengthened.

We were created for this! As believers, redeemed through salvation, we are children of God, choosing to honor His commandments and walk in the authority given through Jesus, the Christ. Accepting the redemption and power received through the shedding blood of Jesus as He bore the pain to ransom our lives, we courageously profess our faith in His name through the circumstances of life.

I can testify in the name of Jesus the blindness I once walked in related to the poor choices in life now challenged by the vision I received through a life with Christ. Understanding the pitfalls of my personal journey, I love you too much not to be honest related to the toxic relationship you continue to walk in, hoping for a future you will not experience. Our testimonies serve the purpose of strengthening our sisters and brothers to overcome through Christ (Revelation 12:11). What didn't kill us has made us strong and fortified our faith in the power of our creator. Yes, it rains on the just and unjust (Matthew 5:45), but I can confidently say, I've seen my Father move mountains to save me.

Our testimonies and worship stand as altars of gratitude unto the Father. Every time that family member, friend, coworker, stranger, or neighbor experiences distressing trials, we can share how we got over through Christ, who strengthens us. We are extensions of the power of His light to transform anyone from darkness (Ephesians 5:8). He found me in the darkest places of my life and loved me unconditionally. Those experiences became my reference points, sowing into the brokenness of others, understanding that our Father is no respecter of persons and would do for them what He has done for me (Acts 10:34). We are His masterpieces, invaluable and daily perfected in the Father's presence to be showcased on life's stage (Ephesians 2:10). Our lives are purposeful in fulfilling the divine assignments we were predestined to accomplish. We were created for this!

Enlarge my territory

When faced with opportunity in the midst of challenges, the perception will distinguish the actions of individuals guiding the course of their destiny. We often watch the lives of others inspired by their accomplishments with the hope of one day walking into our next level. Before it can be, we must first examine what we see for ourselves and have the capacity to believe.

An eagle is said to have one of the strongest eyesights in the animal kingdom, with the ability to spot a rabbit two miles away. You will often hear the phrase "eagle eye," describing a person with keen sight, having the ability to carefully examine and observe particular things and quality. Before Jeremiah was ever used by God, He had to believe in the power of God's touch on his life (Jeremiah 1:9) and receive the supernatural ability to see as the Lord sees (Jeremiah

1:11–13). This is the distinguishing factor of blessed people, yet only a few walk in God's overflow.

In the book of Exodus, the children of Israel experienced the love and supernatural power of God to deliver them from captivity, including the parting of an entire sea (Exodus 14:21). Even through that, they still didn't have the capacity to see the sovereignty of God, possessing no constraints or limits.

If I can reflect back, I can recall the multiple times God stepped in during grave challenges and did the impossible on my behalf yet found myself back on the same path of destruction. We tend to revert back to the familiar, intimidated by our ability to sustain the opportunity before us.

In the book of Numbers, chapter 13, verse 2, God instructs His servant Moses to send out men representing the twelve tribes of Israel to spy out the land of Canaan, which He states He will give them. After a forty-day journey, the men returned to give their report of the promise land God spoke of flowing with milk and honey. Although they viewed the fruitful blessings flowing in the land, ten of the twelve men who made that journey were paralyzed with fear considering the opposition they witnessed in the territory. The leaders Moses and Aaron appointed over the people even fell to their faces as a result of the report (Numbers 14:5). It would leave only Joshua and Caleb of the group of spies confident in the ability of God to give them possession of the land, urging the people to not succumb to fear leading to rebellion against God (Numbers 14:7–9).

Our sight is coupled with the condition of the heart to love and honor God and courageously accept His Word and promises with confidence in the final outcome. We can be in and around the church for years yet without the revelation of what it means to walk in redemption and be the prized possessions of our Father, lacking no good thing.

Based on the condition of their hearts and deficiencies of their mind, the adults who journeyed with Joshua and Caleb would spend forty years wandering in the wilderness without entering into the promise of God. Even the leader Moses would see the promises of

God from a distance without the opportunity to enter (Deuteronomy 32:52).

After gaining revelation through the Word of God, my prayer daily is to push past unbelief so that I may not hinder the divine plans God has for my life. He is bigger than any challenge, obstacle, and perceived setback. In many instances, my natural mind has challenged my faith by evoking thoughts of "what if," "how could you" do this thing. I've now learned the importance of silencing those thoughts by speaking back what the Word of God said I am, what I can do, and all I can have.

If we choose to honor Him by the faith and obedience we walk in, we, too, will experience our promise. The setbacks and delays all have to do with us and the decisions we make based on our understanding. If we are to lead our families as Joshua did, we must adhere to God's instructions. The Father requires that we are strong and courageous through the Word of God, which produces supernatural faith and divine reverence (Joshua 1:8–9). Our territories are enlarged, possessing all we can see by the power of God working in us.

Faith is seen

Before we can experience destiny, we must first see ourselves there. The vision boards regularly created by individuals are designed to expand the capacity to reach the desired destination. As Christians, it's breaking down the self-imposed glass ceiling that causes us to lean solely on our abilities to get it done. Am I ready to defy the mental and spiritual gravity keeping me from getting out of the boat and walking on water?

I've never been a fan of the gym or working out. Over the past year, I saw a reflection that concerned me: a woman who had disregarded the importance of health in finishing this marathon called life. Dr. Kappy, a gifted young doctor of Haitian descent is passionate about a healthy lifestyle. She started me off to a great start on healthy living that prepared my mind and body for the journey ahead. My family became inspired by my journey, and nine-year-old daughters became my junior coaches, helping to ensure the supplements were taken daily, calorie intake logged, and monitored choices I made throughout the day. We started jogging together and establishing family workout sessions led by my husband, Cliff.

Pretty soon, I ran into my girlfriend Angela, a friend and someone I worked out with ten years ago. As we began small group sessions with other women, I was challenged the first day to complete box jumps in the rotation of exercises outlined for the day. As I viewed the box and the height I needed to jump, I didn't even attempt the exercise. Instead, I would do an alternative step up. The more I was consistent with attending the workout sessions, the stronger I became spiritually, mentally, and physically. I would ask the Holy Spirit for help, speak the Word of God while performing the challenge given to complete. After week 5, I became more confident doing box jumps and understood that I always had the ability to complete the exercise once my mental capacity stretched to see myself do what was required.

In the midst of storms and trials, we are susceptible to fear that hinders our progress. In Matthew 14, the disciples were in a small boat in the middle of the sea during a windy and stormy night. They would see the silhouette of a person walking on the water and were terrified by the possibilities of encountering a ghost. The image was Jesus, and He would say to them, "Take courage, it is I; do not be afraid" (Matthew 14:26–27).

It was then that the disciple Peter said to Him, "Lord if it is You, command me to come to You on the water" (verse 28).

As Jesus instructed Peter to come, he would get out of the boat and experience the ability in Christ to walk on water. Although he allowed fear of the wind to stop his progress forward, by getting out of the boat and seeing his ability to walk on water, it expanded his possibilities through Christ Jesus. Peter would go on to accomplish great and mighty works in the name of the Lord, having seen through his many experiences with Christ the assurance found in God.

Faith without works is simply dead (James 2:26). If we sincerely trust the God that is within us, we, too, must take the steps to exercise our faith that leads to the manifestation of the power of Christ in our lives. As Christ's disciples, we have the opportunity each day to witness to others by the life we lead, the courage to persevere, and walk in the authority received in the name of Jesus. Our time spent in church services and watching Christian programs serve the purpose of strengthening each other to go back out and impact the world. We become an extension of faith and the power of God to deliver, heal, and transform.

Building your ark with no signs of rain

There are those who watch my life and hold me in high regard and wouldn't necessarily associate me with the life I've experienced. I tend to laugh and meditate on the power of grace to those that get to a point of being frustrated with complacency when you feel in your spirit that there is more. I pushed past my reality, not because of great confidence and innate abilities but the wholehearted desire to honor the will of my Father, trusting the instructions provided. Only God deserves the glory for all that has transpired in me. He is a covenant-keeping God, who wants His children to experience His very best. Obedience to His instruction is the prerequisite for divine safety, favor, abundance, and acceleration. What I love about my Father is He doesn't disqualify based on multiple mistakes, bad decisions, upbringing, age, race, or educational level. A contrite heart that sincerely repents and is receptive to honoring Him with the life provided will secure the success of your future.

Noah, at the age of five hundred would receive instructions from God to build an ark to preserve his life, the life of his family, and the animals God instructed him to gather because there was a devastating flood coming (Genesis 6:17–19). There had never been rain on the earth, yet God was instructing Noah to do what seemed crazy at five hundred years old with no large group or organization to support the assignment (Genesis 2:5–6).

What's the ark God has instructed you to build? In my solitude with my Father, I honor and thank Him often for not giving up on me. I've seen the instructions provided that He promised to preserve and elevate me but was stuck based on my own thinking and lack of discipline. Like Noah, our obedience has life-changing implications, and we must defy the natural odds to experience His supernatural power. The deeper the walk, the quicker the obedience.

Having learned from numerous (or countless) mistakes, I deeply trust the Holy Spirit, understanding that my trust must yield movement. As I'm building the capacity to respond to the request of the Father, there is a need to be sensitive to what I see, hear, and speak. The more I spend time in the Word of God, reading the power of God in ordinary people, the more my vision increases, my ears become sensitive to what I hear, and my language and posture begin to change.

You will be tested beyond your natural capacity and have to view yourself from the lens of God, deciding to push past insecurities to flow freely in His anointing to accomplish the divine assignment given. Our ark is the bridge to our family's deliverance, the impact we want to see in our communities, and the peace and security found in the Father's presence. The Holy Spirit is right there with us, reaffirming that with God, absolutely nothing shall be impossible (Luke 1:37). It is in the presence of the Holy Spirit that we begin to lay the foundation for what is to come even when we have not yet seen it in natural circumstances.

Chapter 14

SOMEONE IS WATCHING

Strengthen those watching

Our children have front-row seats watching our lives and what it means to be a Christian. They have seen the trials, setbacks, failures, development, reconciliation, promotion, and divine acceleration. I learned from the impact on their lives the importance of open communication, asking for forgiveness, knowing that we can inadvertently wound others, teaching from mistakes so they do not become the norm, cultivating a lifestyle of prayer that embraces repentance and the leading of the Holy Spirit to guide the lives we live.

The stories in the Bible come alive by the experiences we shared and the courage to trust God in every situation faced. We give God the glory He deserves for the giftings we possess, the favor shown, the promotion received, the love that protects, preserves, and encompasses us. We understand that in our natural strength, we lack the capacity to holistically win in every area of life. As His children, we can run into the arms of the Father, acknowledging just where we are and experience His grace, wisdom, healing, and understanding released upon our lives.

To our astoundment, our son Jeremiah, by the age of seven, asked to be publicly baptized because he loved God and wanted Him to know how much he appreciated Him. His twin sisters present at his baptism would request to also be baptized three years later at the age of seven. By the grace of God, we contribute to the decisions and direction those watching take in their own lives.

As Jesus walked the earth, the acts of healing and provision performed in the presence of the disciples revealed the possibilities in God. There were over five thousand who followed Jesus on foot into a desolate area, and He healed their sick (Matthew 14:13–14). The hour was now late, and the disciples were concerned about the feeding of the people and sought to send them to the villages for food.

It was in that place that Jesus took the only five loaves of bread and two fish, and as He looked up to heaven from which all blessings flow, there was an abundance of food to feed the crowd with surplus remaining (Matthew 14:19–21). Jesus knew the hour would come that He would no longer walk the earth with the disciples. He stated, "Truly, truly, I say to you, he who believes in Me, the works that I do, he will do also; and greater works than these will he do; because I go to the Father" (John 14:12).

I look into the eyes of my children and see the joy, giftings, and greatness that lie within. They are living epistles of the unmerited grace that comes from the Father. As I see glimpses of the future that lies before them, I'm led by the Holy Spirit on how to individually love, challenge, and discipline them so that they may maximize the destiny that lies ahead. The foundational factor in the lives of our children is their acceptance of Jesus as Lord of their lives and the incorruptible fact that they can do all things through Christ, who strengthens them (Philippians 4:13). Is this any different for us, the children of God?

Throughout the Bible, we see the supernatural power that comes over believers who choose to humble themselves and inquire of the Lord who brings elevation, deliverance, and a way of escape through the courage and trust we decide to exemplify. How do we get to the place of unwavering trust in the Holy Spirit dwelling within us, prepared to magnify His supernatural power through our lives (1 John 4:4)?

The Father, our Creator, knows us better than we know ourselves. Based on the current state of mind, stamina, resolve, character, and experiences that have left an imprint on our lives influencing our decision-making, reasoning, love walk, ambitions, focus, and courage, there are mountains and valleys required to bring us on the other side of His glory. The life of King David stands as a personal reference point of childlike faith that overwhelmingly elevates (David and Goliath), guides character building in your wilderness (ability to kill Saul in a cave), demonstrates the abuse of power (David killed Uriah for Bathsheba), impact of generational curse unaddressed (Absalom trying to kill his father and David knowing his own sin), and power of heartfelt repentance and reconciliation (David returns to the Father through prayer).

As we've seen in the Bible and in our own personal stories, there's always someone watching. Are those seeing the demonstration of our lives comforted in complaining, lacking, and accepting of spiritual and physical bondage? Have we exemplified the character and strength that inspire greatness through a trusting relationship with the Holy Spirit? The levels of freedom and victory available in our walk with God are unlimited and all-encompassing. Let's choose to surrender our will and way to the Father and allow the Holy Spirit to steer the ship to victory that ignites our greater level and inspires the lives of those present.

Our children are now thirteen and ten. Their capacity to walk by faith is astounding. As they watched their parents push through and accomplish goals that stretched us, their faith grew to the point that they now speak to their future and pray for their healing, knowing that the authority of Christ is in them. During our family time of prayer and thanksgiving, they regularly share the move of God in their lives and the answer to prayers they received when they activated faith in the situations faced. It is never too early to lay the groundwork of understanding that brings clarity to the path of success. There are situations experienced that I desired to teach from to help my children and others avoid the pitfalls I endured. Faith exercised demonstrates the way that leads to truth and abundant life.

Chapter 15

OUR INHERITANCE

The kingdom

We, the people, perish because of a lack of knowledge and revelation, which impacts how we see ourselves and how we function in life. As people rebirthed spiritually through Christ, we are not conformed to this world but transformed by the renewal of our mind, progressively maturing in our focus of godly values and ethical attitudes so that we demonstrate the perfect and acceptable will of God (Romans 12:2). As believers, Jesus stated,

> My kingdom is not of this world. If my kingdom were of this world, my servants would have been fighting, that I might not be delivered over to the Jews. But my kingdom is not from the world. (John 18:36)

In order to live victoriously through Christ, we must walk in the revelation and understanding of what it means to be citizens of the kingdom of God. Although all kingdoms have the proceeding components, the sovereignty of God Almighty can never be compared to the kingdoms of this world. *Kingdom* defined is governance by a king over identified territory, where his dominion or lordship is exercised, impacting the lives of its citizens (KingdomCitizens.org). A king receives his position through birthright and not the consensus of the people. According to KindomCitizens.org, to be a kingdom, the following must be present:

- **The king**: the embodiment of the kingdom, representing its glory and nature through foremost authority and lordship.
- **The territory**: encompasses the domain owned by the king, inclusive of the resources and people where his lordship is exercised.
- **The constitution**: conveys the mind and will of the king concerning the citizens.
- **The citizenry**: people privileged to live under the rule of the king, where he fulfills his obligation to care for and protect those under his authority.
- **The law**: the administration established through the standards and principles developed by the king, guaranteeing access to benefits of the kingdom. The law is irrevocable and nondebatable by citizens.
- **The privileges**: citizenship comes with the assurance of the king's protection and provision.
- **A code of ethics**: citizens are ambassadors who represent the moral standards, social relationships, personal conduct, attitude, attire, and manner of life of the kingdom.
- **The army**: system established by the kingdom to secure the territory and protect its citizens. Citizens are not enlisted in the army but receive its protection.
- **A commonwealth**: all citizens are afforded equal access to financial security through its economic system.
- **The social culture**: expression of the king's nature through the lifestyle of his citizens.

The kingdom of God

As children of light, we have entered a divine kingdom through the confession of Jesus, the Christ, as Lord of our lives, for He is the King of kings and Lord of lords (Revelation 19:16). We are now citizens of the kingdom of God, clothed in royalty and covered by the King's written Word found in the Bible to guide, protect, provide, and empower. Through His covenant constitution known as the Word of God, He has given us the vast territory of this world (Joshua 1:3–4), safety in every circumstance faced (2 Chronicles 20:15), with great expectation (1 Corinthians 2:9). His asks: seek first His kingdom and His righteousness that you may lack no need and be in a place of peace (Matthew 6:33).

When we seek God's kingdom, we are focused on Him and not what this world has to offer, understanding that all belongs to Him (Psalm 24:1) and He does not desire to withhold anything good from us. When His kingdom is first in our hearts and the lives we live, we want to do what is right in His sight, allowing for adjustments in our attitudes and pruning of our character.

I have watched many good people with potential accelerate to the top but found themselves spiraling down while calling on the name of the Lord. The King in this kingdom introspectively examines the heart, motives, and character. Am I sincerely spending time in the presence of God daily, allowing the Holy Spirit to gently help me make the adjustments necessary in my character and focus that produce a sustainable blessed life in the presence of the Father? The mistakes I've made in life have helped me to gauge the areas of growth necessary to maximize my inheritance as a kingdom citizen. Consistent battles with fornication, lust, lies, unforgiveness, poor stewardship over money, position, and family were indicators that the kingdom of God was not first in my life, for we cannot seek His kingdom first and remain lacking, bound, and defeated.

The kingdom of God is a matter of the heart with boundless territory. My family and I regularly encounter great opportunities for financial wealth and promotion. We ask now, after all we've endured, Father, if it be Your will, open the door and bless us abundantly. If not, please close the door to the opportunity before us. We have lived to experience the fullness of joy in the will of God and the power of His divine presence and guidance. We, the church, are under the lordship of Christ with blessed assurance. It is our responsibility to not substitute His presence and divine guidance for religious activities that yield no power.

The kingdom of God is at hand (Matthew 4:17) for a divided and hurting world. Our approach must reflect the compassionate love of Christ that welcomes and respects all people, loving them as we would love ourselves (Matthew 22:38–39). We cannot give what we do not have. The love we first need to receive is in the Father's presence exemplified through the love expressed by our King, Jesus, a love that surrendered to death on behalf of the people desired to save. As citizens of the kingdom of God, it is our responsibility to represent our King well that those living on the outskirts may experience the true essence of the King of kings, who authentically reveals His agape love that they may desire to enter in.

Entrusted with the scepter: authority through the Word of God

I was raised in environments that required tough skin and combative posture to survive. Retaliation against attacks was necessary to avoid being continuously victimized. I was used to fighting for myself and my family, and I learned to trust very few. Surrender was a sign of weakness and vulnerability. It was essential to assess the stipulations associated with good deeds done for me to avoid greater loss.

Here I am, a woman taught to be physically and mentally tough, introduced to a God who came in the flesh to endure persecution, ridicule, physical harm to the point of death that He may redeem my life and invite me into His everlasting kingdom of safety, liberation, health, abundance, and peace. How do I respond, considering my state of mind? For the thought of the One who knew no sin willing to die that I may live challenged my beliefs, causing a raging battle in my mind (2 Corinthians 5:21). The cost: humbly accept the need to be saved and redeemed from the bondage that encapsulated my life in an invisible prison. Receiving the lordship of Christ Jesus and the authority He extended as a woman made the righteousness of God, not through the acts I performed but the choice of Jesus, the Christ, as Lord of my life.

As an earthly king holds his scepter as a symbol of power and authority, Jesus, the King of all kings and Lord of all lords, has extended His authority to us as ambassadors of the kingdom of God on earth. Dr. Tony Evans defines *kingdom authority* as the divinely delegated right and responsibility for believers to act on God's behalf in spiritually ruling His creation under the lordship of Jesus Christ. Through the authority we have in Christ, we hold the keys to the kingdom of heaven that whatever we bind on earth will be bound in heaven, and whatever we loose on earth, will also be loosed in heaven (Matthew 16:19). Sickness, disease, failing schools, unstable government, distressed environments, defective portrayal in arts and entertainment cannot stand if we confidently call on the name of Jesus and speak His Word and promises over the conditions of life.

Know this: faith without works is dead (James 2:14). The very things that keep you up at night and disturb your heart and spirit are awaiting your impact. When we receive and act in our roles as ambassadors carrying the authority of Christ, change and transformation come, for Jesus is the light of the world, and we carry His light into every dark place, shattering the strongholds of depression, lack, sickness, and oppression (John 8:12).

The past does not have the power to disqualify you from the life God desires for you. For Jesus, the Son of God, seated at the right of the throne, endured the cross, bearing every sin and disease of those that received Him as Lord (Hebrews 12:2). Our slate was washed clean with the opportunity to confidently start over again, throwing every mistake into the sea of forgetfulness. Through Jesus, the Christ, we are made the righteousness of God (2 Corinthians 5:21).

Righteousness is established through an unfailing relationship of love, honor, and respect between a believer and our heavenly advocate Jesus. Righteous people have right standing in the eyes of God. Like a child who desires to make their parents and older siblings proud, we extend our gratitude to the Father daily for the saving grace provided through Jesus that we consciously are receptive to the need to develop in character, conduct, and faith.

Gideon, scared of loss, would have never experienced the power of God if he remained hiding from his enemies (Judges 6). Through the Lordship of Jesus, the Father is calling us by name to get into our rightful position that we may exercise the power and authority we carry as sons and daughters of the Most High God. If we remain dormant and paralyzed by fear of the unknown, we can never fully enter into the abundant promises of God nor the assignments associated with our lives.

God is not looking for perfect people, for we have all fallen short. He's looking for those who will believe Him to do the impossible in their lives, shattering all perceived limitations (Luke 1:45), for we are the ambassadors of Jesus, the Christ, deployed with His authority to speak to the challenges of life and expect divine victory. The victory was secured through Jesus our Lord. He has made us righteous. We live a life of righteousness through an unfailing relationship of love, honor, and respect between a believer and heavenly advocate Jesus. It's time to firmly walk in our divine authority.

Daughters of the King

> The king answered Daniel and said, "Surely your God is the God of gods and a Lord of kings and a revealer of mysteries, since you have been able to reveal this mystery." (Daniel 2:47)

Greater is He who is in you than he who is in the world (1 John 4:4). You are the answer to the world's problems by the Spirit of God who is operating in you. You have been anointed and appointed to go into the world, representing your Father with all confidence. Know that the life and the experiences that you have endured and developed through now stand as stepping stones for your ability to compassionately relate, lead, guide, and help bring forth wisdom and understanding. You carry the answer to problems of this world that will shift communities and transform the lives of others. Your pain, your deliverance, your suffering will serve a divine purpose. It molded the leader, the woman of great resolve and resilience, a woman who doesn't just sit with the Father in the kingdom but compassionately moves the priorities of the kingdom forward.

We are daughters of the King. Everything that you have endured didn't come to kill you, but it strengthened you to confidently lead through the Spirit of the Lord operating in you. A daughter of the King confidently cultivates and speaks with divine wisdom. Like Daniel, in the book of Daniel, chapter 2, God will elevate you amongst people. He will distinguish you through His Spirit who is operating in your life. The world will know of the God who is within you, for you will be distinguished in all of the lands. You will bring forth the answer to the world's problems.

You are seated amongst leaders as an influencer in family, ministry, education, business, government, media, and arts. You're called to break down strongholds as a woman who walks in the authority of Jesus, bringing forth light in dark places. The divine providence of God is upon you as His daughter on the earth, defying every impossibility. You lack no good thing, for the peace of the Father and His supernatural abilities magnify your impact. As His ambassador, you are well dressed for every occasion, having raged war in your prayer closet and emerged with confidence, wearing that outfit and stilettos. You are unapologetically you! Confident in the One who has made you for such a time, shine brightly, for you are daughters of the King!

Divinely orchestrated

Through the process of writing this book, I called my biological father to learn more about my grandfather, whom I never had the opportunity to meet, yet whom so many admired. Although I knew my grandfather—the late James Y. Gbarbea Sr. was the first superintendent of Bong County in Liberia, equivalent to the governor of a state in our American governmental structure—I never knew the extent of his legacy. He was a well-educated man with a servant's heart. His contributions to the kingdom of God and his beloved Liberia led him to serve as one of the two translators of the

Bible in the Kpelle dialect, spoken by the Kpelle people, the largest indigenous African tribe in the country. He labored for all humanity, ensuring that people in rural areas had access to opportunities. As the first Rural Area Development (RAD) administrator, he established community development in the interior sectors, which brought infrastructure and schools to Nimba and Bong counties.

Through these efforts, the First Lutheran Church was established in the county, and the late James Y. Gbarbea Sr. became affectionately known as the "father of Bong County." His work led him to serve as a contributor to the writing of the 1986 New Constitution that established a more efficient government and elevated the voice and inclusion of the rural (interior people) into the country's mainstream. His efforts made a lasting impact on the country and brought forth persecution that led to imprisonment. God searches the heart and motives of man. In the book of Genesis, chapter 22, verse 18, He declared over Abraham, "In your seed, all nations of the earth shall be blessed, because you have heard and obeyed My voice."

If anyone had attempted to chart my future trajectory by simply looking at my birth and the early experiences of my life, it would be far from encouraging. Understand, Jesus paid the ultimate price for us and, through His unfailing love, sent others before us to prepare the way by courageously tilling the soil deeply for the planting of seeds watered generationally for the establishment of legacy. The conditions that we face in life impact the process of our growth and the development of our faith. The end product is undoubtedly beautiful if we can endure through the challenge of the elements and our process of development to live out God's intended outcome. The journey is real.

Twenty years ago, in my early twenties, I saw myself on a large stage, preparing to speak to a sea of people. The vision frightened me, considering the life that I lived. How could I envision such a thing? I chose to drown that thought in the sea of forgetfulness, thinking myself unqualified to stand and lead. There was a time in my life that I was so insecure that even being in a room where others could observe me and examine my imperfections intimidated me, yet I'm dreaming of standing before thousands?

I'm reminded today that without surrendering our will and understanding to the Father, we will never experience destiny, for His thoughts are not my thoughts and His ways are not my ways (Isaiah 55:8). Like my brother Jonah, the mandate received from the Lord was to bring guidance to the course of my life, yet based on religion, culture, experiences, poor examples, and beliefs, we find ourselves running in the opposite direction of destiny (Jonah 1:1–3). We limit our lives and all those we are connected to by not courageously developing in obedience, compassionate love for the Father, skills for the assignment, and trust in our Creator.

Jonah experienced trials and setbacks that should have killed him, but the Father's unfailing mercies were always there ready to receive him. In verse 2 of chapter 2, Jonah declared, "I called out of my distress to the Lord, and He answered me. I cried for help from the depths of sheol [hell]; You heard my voice." I am grateful to God each day that He knows the road that His children take and chooses to extend His helping hand to pull us out of our pits of despair and get us back on course.

Twenty years ago, I started running after seeing an impossible dream. I wasn't able to see what He saw and didn't want to fail. Mistake after mistake, I cried and got back up again. In the midst of my pain, I didn't even realize the spiritual and physical strength developing in me. I experienced unimaginable forgiveness that erased my past. Why would I then hold unforgiveness toward others?

My life experiences began to become a reference point of the possibilities in God. Like David, when recalling his ability to kill the lion and bear that came against his father's livestock (1 Samuel 17:34–36), I know the power of God's anointing to shatter strongholds, dismantle the plans of the enemy, and restore what was lost by the authority found in the name of Jesus. After seeing that vision from God, it took twenty years of my life to get to the doors of destiny. I realize now that not one day was wasted. I needed the twenty years of preparation and training to become the woman I was predestined to be. My daughters and the many women I encounter will accelerate in their process, learning from my life, which is now an open reference point to those who desire to live a victorious life in the presence of the Father.

Jonah completed his divine assignment in Nineveh, causing over one hundred thousand people to be saved from the wrath of God (Jonah 3). Embrace your process and experience the power of God as a daughter of the King to lead by example, walking in the power and authority of your Father. Without ever physically meeting my grandfather, the late James Y. Gbarbea Sr. was sowing into the destiny of his bloodline by obeying the voice of God. As my maternal grandfather, the late George Marsh radically turned to God in his later years; he, too, made divine deposits for the legacy that was to be created. From the mouth and laying on of hands from the late Elizabeth Barclay-Marsh, my maternal grandmother, and the beloved Jerusha "Ma Titi" Jallah, my paternal grandmother, I received deposits of blessings birthed out of their journey with God. My life was divinely orchestrated for such a time.

My prayer for the reader today is that you introspectively examine your life, considering your dreams, condition of your soul, family, and destiny. If you have accepted Jesus as Lord of your life, are you experiencing an unspeakable joy in the midst of all life brings that delivers, heals, sustains, and elevates? If not, it's time to find a quiet place and commit the time in His presence to reveal to you so that He may redeem you from bondage.

You see, Mephibosheth, which means "from the mouth of shame," was born into royalty, yet at the age of five, both his grandfather King Saul and father Jonathan were killed in the war, and while his nurse hastily fled with him, she dropped him, and he became crippled in his feet (2 Samuel 4:4). As an adult, he lived in Lo-Debar, which means "no pasture" and soon viewed himself as a "dead dog" (2 Samuel 9:4–8). If our circumstances steal our focus and become our identity, we stop living. The fact that you are still here after all life has hit you with should fuel your capacity to embrace the divine plan for your tomorrow. The Father, in His sovereignty, wants to deliver you from the mouth of shame and give you divine beauty for your ashes.

King David restored to Mephibosheth all the land of his grandfather King Saul and provided him a regular seat at the table in his palace (2 Samuel 9:7). Our heavenly Father desires to restore His daughters back to their rightful place in the kingdom, armed with the authority they possess in Jesus (scepter) and divine leading of the Holy Spirit.

I learned, and I confess, and I share with you today that with God, all things are possible (Matthew 19:26). He can dry every tear and deliver you from the pains of your past. He can set you up high and preserve you in your position. He can bless your womb with children, even when the report is bleak while restoring your home and marriage. The questions of my life had nothing to do with the abilities of a Father who created the heavens and the earth but rather my willingness to surrender to my divine process.

The trials and temptations didn't come to destroy me but helped me become who I was already created to be. Like you, I have been impacted by this world yet not of it (Romans 12:2). So we have to go through a process of being refined and purified that we may walk in the image, the likeness, and character of our Father, who is in heaven and dwells in our hearts in the form of the Holy Spirit (1 John 4:4). It's time that you sit in your seat of authority as a daughter of the King.

Michelle Davidson is a life strategist, certified Christian life coach, entrepreneur, and featured author in the Amazon international bestseller Voices of the 21st Century: Resilient Women Who Rise and Make a Difference. She is the proud wife of Cliff Davidson and mother to Ndiaye and miracle children Jeremiah, Destiny Grace, and Danielle Joy.